"Dan Burke's new book is a powerful reminder that there is a battle for the salvation of our souls. In this book, he explains the teachings of the great mystical saints to help you understand what you can do to win the battle, grow closer to Christ, and achieve the peace that only He can give you. I recommend this book for anyone ready to grow in holiness."

—Cardinal Gerhard Müller
Former Prefect of the Congregation
for the Doctrine of the Faith

"Dan Burke's new book provides essential, inspired formation for equipping the Church Militant. Many people who read and practice the Spiritual Exercises articulated here in a new light will be prepared to overcome personal and corporate sin and evil. I expect this work to inspire a movement of aspiring saints, fierce soldiers for Christ!"

—Kathleen Beckman, Diocese of Orange, California
Deliverance, Exorcism Ministry Coordinator

"As Christians, we have received the vocation to holiness, but we need the guidance of the Holy Spirit. We also need human support. This book offers us much wisdom from the spiritual tradition of the Church. I hope and pray that many faithful will be helped by this book on their spiritual journey."

—Cardinal Anders Arborelius, O.C.D.
Bishop of Stockholm

"Dan Burke has become a wonderful conveyer of the deep wisdom of the saints in language that is easy to understand. He does it again in this book. What a wonderful introduction to the basic principles of discernment! And how important discernment is!"

—Dr. Ralph Martin
Author, *The Fulfillment of All Desire*

"Since believing God's word is essential to victory in battles of the spiritual life, knowing how to discern His word is nonnegotiable. In this profound little book, Dan Burke puts on display, for all to see, the clarifying power of the Ignatian spiritual tradition in helping us discern the movements of the heart. The insights and explanations on how to apply the wisdom of St. Ignatius in this book will equip readers to know the voice of God more clearly and help them detect and root out the deceptions of the enemy. For those who want to live in victory over the enemy, I heartily recommend this book!"

—Fr. Mathias Thelen
President of Encounter Ministries
Brighton, Michigan

"Dan Burke has given us a personal, practical, lucid, and easily accessible path into the rules for discernment of spirits provided by St. Ignatius Loyola and taught by the Avila Institute. He illuminates the meaning of alternations between consolation and desolation, in deepening humility, surrendering to grace and dependence on God."

—Fr. Tom Acklin
Director of Counseling, St. Vincent Seminary

Spiritual Warfare and the Discernment of Spirits

Dan Burke

Spiritual Warfare
and the
Discernment
of Spirits

SPIRITUAL DIRECTION
SERIES

SOPHIA INSTITUTE PRESS

Manchester, New Hampshire

Nihil Obstat: Fr. Bryan W. Jerabek, J.C.L.
Censor Librorum

Imprimatur: + Robert J. Baker, S.T.D.
Bishop of Birmingham in Alabama
February 11, 2020, Our Lady of Lourdes

Sophia Institute Press
Box 5284, Manchester, NH 03108
1-800-888-9344

www.SophiaInstitute.com

Sophia Institute Press® is a registered trademark of Sophia Institute.

ISBN 978-1-64413-257-9

Library of Congress Control Number:2019954529

8th printing

To Stephanie Burke:
thank you for the years of valiant battle
against sin and for God

Contents

Foreword

Stop and ask yourself: Why did I buy this book? What am I looking for? What problem do I hope to solve? What correct decision do I hope to be able to make? What bad decision do I hope to be able to rectify? It might be another reason, but *stop*! Know what you are looking for and vocalize it to yourself — write it down.

Now ask God, in the power of the Holy Spirit living inside you, to lead you to the specific wisdom in this book that is the key that unlocks what treasure you seek. Make that same Holy Spirit prayer each time you pick up the book and commence reading it.

Make this exact prayer each morning when you wake up: "Holy Spirit, lead me to the wisdom today that unlocks the path to God's will for me in the large and small choices of my life so that in all my thoughts, words, and deeds, I might give glory to God." If you do this, you have consciously chosen to live a life of discernment.

We need these tools and rules of spiritual warfare, because whether life has been a bowl of cherries or a bed of nails, our human nature, crafted in the Divine Image, has been shattered by Original Sin. Without the road map that such rules and tools provide, we will not safely find our way home to Eternal Life in the Kingdom of the Father.

Spiritual Warfare and the Discernment of Spirits

As Dan Burke writes in this short primer, learning the tools and rules of discernment minimizes the wounds of early life — of our human nature — that create the spiritual tinnitus of anxiety. Left "untreated," we are overcome with our burdens and thus susceptible to the despair that Satan desires while missing the grace, healing, and love God offers us in our time of need.

For those of you new to the practice of spiritual discernment, Dan Burke's book will be a revelation. You will awaken to knowing more surely the difference between the light and the darkness. For those of you who are more proficient in discernment, the book will be a reminder — specifically, that at the deeper levels of spiritual maturity, what seems to be light can actually be fool's gold, and what feels like darkness can be true gold.

Those Christians who choose to engage in spiritual warfare on the battlefield of their souls and in our world at this climactic time in the third millennium, are the soldiers Christ needs *now*! Carry this battle primer with you, and don't be afraid of what is to come. Remember the words of our leader, Christ Jesus: "And when he comes he will convict the world in regard to sin and righteousness and condemnation: sin, because they do not believe in me; righteousness, because I am going to the Father and you will no longer see me; condemnation, because the ruler of this world has been condemned.... I have told you this so that you might have peace in me. In the world you will have trouble, but take courage, I have conquered the world" (John 16:8–11, 33, NABRE).

—Fr. William Watson, S.J., D.Min.

Preface (and a Promise)

As I reveal in the introduction that follows, my exposure to spiritual battles due to situations in my childhood and the path God has had for me in life have been significant. Later in life I became Catholic, and by God's grace, I discovered a more refined and powerful approach to the daily battle with the enemy of peace in the wisdom of St. Ignatius. The two priests to whom I owe a great debt in this study are Fathers Timothy Gallagher, O.M.V., and William Watson, S.J. Both of these men are scholars and provide many in-depth pathways into the wisdom of the warfare of St. Ignatius and the peace that comes when we learn how to fight. In contrast, but also in correspondence to their in-depth works, my intent in this book is to provide a very personal, simple, and practical introduction to these powerful paths of peace and spiritual growth. My hope is that this quick read will encourage you to begin to delve into this life-changing wisdom and that you will then explore the deeper waters in the invaluable works of both Fr. Gallagher and Fr. Watson. Ultimately, my prayer is that you will know the peace that Jesus has prepared for you in and through the warfare that you are called to engage in.

The only thing I will offer further is this promise: If you give yourself to God, learn to fight the battle of life on His terms, you will find the peace that Jesus has promised — the peace that transcends all understanding.

—Dan Burke
October 15, 2019
Feast of St. Teresa of Avila

Spiritual Warfare and the
Discernment of Spirits

Introduction: Out of the Darkness

But you are a chosen race, a royal priesthood, a holy nation,
God's own people, that you may declare the wonderful deeds of
him who called you out of darkness into his marvelous light.

—1 Peter 2:9

I emerged out of the darkness of my youth through coming to
know Jesus the Messiah. In coming to faith, I also came to experience hope for the first time in my life. However, coming to
know peace was elusive and a much longer process. As a young
man, I recall struggling with Jesus' assurances about the peace
He gives and the many other promises in the New Testament
about peace. I just couldn't figure out how to lay hold of that
peace or how to experience it.

My childhood was a constant emotional tornado. Some
of my siblings didn't make it out alive. Most of those who did
survive have been in and out of drug rehab, attempted suicide,
and live generally destructive patterns of life. Here are a few
scenes out of my youth to give you just a taste of what I lived
through and why anxiety was so easy to come by and peace so
hard to find.

Spiritual Warfare and the Discernment of Spirits

Scene 1: Screaming, rage, another full-volume and frightening argument, and then *boom!* dead silence. A gunshot. I was only nine, but I knew what it was. My two younger brothers and I huddled at the bottom of the stairs, frozen with terror in the eternal silence. Was my mother dead? Would he kill us next? I couldn't move, or run, or think. It seemed like an eternity before we discovered what had happened — although we never really learned the full story.

Scene 2: I was terrified at the twisted thing I had seen calling me. It made no sense. I was home alone, dizzy with fear. It was tormenting me. I had no idea what to do. I was so overcome and irrational that, in my childish fear, I sought to burrow my head into the corner of our couch between the cushions as if trying to escape to where I couldn't be found. Wailing, crying, hysterical. My mother returned home to find me in the delirium. She hit me and yelled at me. No comfort, no attempt to understand why her child was beyond consolation. She brought the demons in through her involvement in the occult. Her response to the wounds and terror she caused was to strike again at her child — at me — as if I was an uncaused annoyance. The confusion was beyond anything a small child could fathom or process. The damage was almost irreversible ... almost.

These two scenes from my youth — not necessarily the worst and most painful ones — were just two in a string of seemingly endless torments until I left home. But the torments didn't stop. Those who have lived through abuse know that it stays with you, the tortured twisting and turning of mind and heart constantly replaying the scenes and the hurt.

Introduction: Out of the Darkness

Some of you can imagine the trauma. For some, much less dramatic suffering has still yielded a deeply wounded heart and mind. It doesn't matter what we have wrestled through or how severe. We could have even grown up in a happy and loving Christian home but still struggle with anxiety. My only point in sharing these details is to give you hope. If I can find peace, it is within the reach of anyone who draws near to God and seeks the eternal remedy that only He can provide. There is hope. You can and will find peace if you seek the peace that He bought and paid for by His own torment and sacrifice on your behalf.

Counterfeit Remedies

For such men are false apostles, deceitful workmen, disguising
themselves as emissaries of Christ. And no wonder, for
even Satan disguises himself as an angel of light.

—2 Corinthians 11:13–14

Before we begin to explore the authentic path to peace, it is worth
a brief reflection on a common barrier to knowing true peace
and getting caught up on counterfeit pathways. The reasons for
the interest in counterfeit pathways are many. Some of them are
rooted in a cultural narcissism, pride, curiosity, and disdain of
anything that is not "new." Some of them are rooted in ignorance
and a lack of understanding of the riches available to us in the
Catholic Faith and mystical tradition.

Many long-time Catholics have a kind of confident pseudo-
knowledge of the faith. Here's how it works. Because they have
heard some basic ideas and have a rudimentary understanding
of them, they believe they understand the entirety of these con-
cepts central to their faith. I have had countless conversations
with Catholics seeking false remedies in New Age and non-
Christian Eastern spiritualities. They usually begin with "I have
been a Catholic all my life, and I have found nothing wrong with

XYZ." The problem is that catechesis in past decades has been horrifyingly vacuous, and most Catholics know almost nothing of substance about their faith. This isn't an overstatement; it is revealed by survey after survey—Catholics simply do not know the Faith they claim. Years of immersion in the shallow end of the pool does not teach someone to swim, no matter how much time they have spent in the water. Such a shaky foundation provides a kind of dangerous confidence that could lead even to eternal peril in the case of those who follow non-Christian Eastern spirituality and get lost in it.

Given this fertile environment, false remedies abound, and charlatans are more than happy to be paid for them. "For just $49.95, you too can have peace!" Even well-formed Catholics can fall into the trap when they don't exercise diligence in vetting the remedies they seek. Mindfulness is the latest fad as of the writing of this book. The saddest aspect of this particular fad is that the scientific world outside of the Catholic Church is already admitting to the spurious claims and practices, while the snake-oil salesmen are still selling and making money and attempting to discredit the cries for sanity among the faithful. Mindfulness will unfortunately have a long life in the Church because it is lucrative to those who sell it, interesting to those who buy it, and because people are desperate for answers.

The other factor that fuels interest in these esoteric "new and exciting" remedies is the human ego. With an underappreciation for the long-successful tradition of healing and spiritual growth of the Catholic Church, we are more than ready to seek the complicated and "scientific" remedies elsewhere. These false remedies are all the more attractive to the orthodox when coupled with the Faith they value. The most popular versions of snake-oil are those combined with what sounds like traditional Catholic spirituality. So we have Buddhism mixed with the Sacrament of the Present Moment as if they are somehow compatible. Of course, Jesus really had shortcomings that only the Buddha can solve. Thus, we must look outside the Church for answers. When it comes to the claims of mindfulness, however, scientific studies do not bear them out. As could have been easily predicted, the suffering of so many coupled with the energetic hype caused a rush into a sloppy analysis and embrace of this and many other false remedies. This is, in part, a repeat of pop-psychology solutions and pop-spirituality of the 1970s when a few well-intentioned but poorly formed priests sought to meet the growing interest in prayer through non-Christian Eastern ideas and Transcendental Meditation. To explore a truly trustworthy treatment of the dangerous fairy-tale world of mindfulness, I would strongly refer you to Susan Brinkman's excellent and well-researched book, *A Catholic Guide to Mindfulness*.[1] As well, you can find statements from prominent Catholic psychologists such as Allison Ricciardi, the head of the Catholic Therapists Association, refuting the practice.[2]

My intent here is not to dwell on mindfulness alone, but to simply warn the desperate reader that just because something is new and popular, has a Catholic label, and you can't find anything wrong with it, doesn't mean there isn't poison in the well. The good news is that Jesus promised us peace, and He has not failed to keep His promise. He doesn't need Buddha to help you find

---

[1]   Susan Brinkman, OCDS, *A Catholic Guide to Mindfulness* (n.p.: CreateSpace, 2017).

[2]   "Mindfulness in Therapy: Is That All There Is?," *National Catholic Register*, April 29, 2019, http://www.ncregister.com/blog/brinkmann/mindfulness-in-therapy-is-that-all-there-is.

peace. The unfailing path to peace that He has provided will be the focus of the remainder of our exploration.

Questions for Reflection

- How would you describe your spiritual formation? How well do you understand the truths of your Catholic faith? Have you read the *Catechism* cover to cover?
- Have you been drawn to any false remedies on your quest for peace and healing? If so, which ones? What has been the result?
- What has been your experience of the peace that Jesus promises?

An Invitation to Healing

*Peace I leave with you; my peace I give to you; not
as the world gives do I give to you. Let not your
hearts be troubled, neither let them be afraid."*

—John 14:27

Whenever events surface that cause us anxiety, they are an invitation from God to healing. They are similar to the warning lights on the dashboards of our cars. They let us know that something is wrong and needs to be remedied.

After I came to Christ as a young man, every light lit up on my dashboard on most days. Because of Jesus, I did have hope, but I was severely lacking in the peace category. I would read passages like John 14:27 and wonder why I didn't have what Jesus promised to give me. After all, I really believed. I was one of those folks who was all in for Jesus. I was at church every time the doors were open. I participated in evangelism and works of service. I read the Bible and prayed every day. Why was my spiritual health dashboard light continuously on — and flashing so bright? Hindsight provides the answer: the Lord was inviting me to be healed.

Spiritual Warfare and the Discernment of Spirits

At some point along the way I was challenged to begin memorizing Scripture. The first twenty passages or so were focused on how to communicate the Gospel—the Good News of Jesus. I noticed that every time I opened up the Bible and sought to bring a passage of Scripture into memory, I encountered a tiny taste of peace—just enough to keep drawing me back into the project. Because of my continued emotional and spiritual suffering, I decided to study suffering in the New Testament. For this project I forced myself to type out every passage in the New Testament about suffering and then categorize each one. As each word inspired by the Holy Spirit entered my mind, my hope increased, and a pattern began to emerge.

This pattern was the constant promise of peace, and in the Holy Spirit-inspired writings of St. Paul, a constant reference to the mind. There were a handful of passages that haunted me, such as Jesus' promise in John 14:27. The first one to hit me was from St. Paul's letter to the Romans:

> I appeal to you therefore, brethren, by the mercies of God, to present your bodies as a living sacrifice, holy and acceptable to God, which is your spiritual worship. Do not be conformed to this world but be transformed by the renewal of your mind, that you may prove what is the will of God, what is good and acceptable and perfect. (Romans 12:1–2)

I looked up the word *transformed* and discovered that in the Greek it is the same word we use to describe the change of a caterpillar into a butterfly—*metamorphosis*. This said to me that my mind could be healed and changed from something that tormented me to something that was beautiful and free. Even so, I had no inkling as to how this could be true in practical terms.

But as God is oft found to do, the seed that He planted soon began to nurture and grow.

The next Holy Spirit-breathed passage that hit me began to shed more light on my quest as I read and studied in earnest. In St. Paul's Second Letter to the Corinthians, he said:

> For though we live in the world we are not carrying on a worldly war, for the weapons of our warfare are not worldly but have divine power to destroy strongholds. We destroy arguments and every proud obstacle to the knowledge of God, and take every thought captive to obey Christ. (2 Corinthians 10:3–5)

So, there is a war. That is clear enough. It was clear in the Gospels. It was clear in my life at that moment. There was and is a war, and that war is between Satan and God's people—of whom I am one. In this passage, St. Paul reveals that we have weapons at our disposal and that they carry the power of God to destroy "strongholds." What was he talking about? I explored these ideas diligently. I discovered that the Greek word used for *strongholds* is also used in Scripture to describe fortresses and military centers of strength occupied or controlled by the enemy of our souls or by the temporal enemies of God's people. So, there are "strongholds" that need to be destroyed, and we have power at our disposal to destroy them—God's power. What are these strongholds?

St. Paul continues, "We destroy arguments and every proud obstacle to the knowledge of God." So then, the strongholds are arguments and proud obstacles to the knowledge of God. It seemed to me that this was a description of a war in the mind. I knew that war well. The way to win the war was to avail myself of the power of God to destroy the lies that the enemy had sown into my mind. Our central strategy, by the power of God, is to take every thought captive—to make them obedient to Christ. But what does that mean?

Well, we have thoughts that are obedient to Christ and those that are disobedient or opposed to Him. Thoughts that are obedient to Christ must be thoughts that are true, and thoughts that are disobedient to Christ must be those that are false or chaotic, that cause anxiety, fear, and disruption of mind and heart.

Things began to make sense. I decided to experiment with this idea of taking thoughts captive. Because of my upbringing, I had many lies in my head about who I was and what my worth was. One of the more painful moments of my childhood was overhearing my mother talking about me to a friend. She said something no child should ever have to hear, and it ripped into my heart. She said, "He is a piece of _____." Mind you, I was somewhere around seven years old and a compliant though very sickly child. I am sure I was a burden in many ways, but I wasn't rebellious or disrespectful at this point. Why would she say this about me? I was crushed. Now, as an adult, I remembered this pain—the lie. Put into more palatable language, the poisonous lie my mother so cruelly injected into my heart was that I was worse than worthless. Unfortunately, this lie was surrounded by a fortress of hundreds more just like it. These pillars that sustained the fortress walls of Satan were all pounded into me by people who were supposed to protect and nurture me. Those lies nearly destroyed me. Now I had hope that they could be defeated.

The "how" wasn't complicated. I remembered that every time Jesus was tempted by Satan in the fourth chapter of St. Matthew's Gospel, He responded with Scripture. Why couldn't I do the same or something similar? The pattern was simple. The devil offered a temptation—a lie—and Jesus responded with the truth. I simply took a piece of paper and folded it in half the long way. On the left side I wrote the heading "Lies I Believe." On the right side I wrote "Truths of God." Here's an example:

Lies I Believe	Truths of God
I am as worthless as a piece of _____.	I am a child of God—John 1:12
	I have been chosen by God and adopted by Him—He set me apart from the beginning of creation—Ephesians 1:3–8

The next step was fueled by a passage in the Letter of St. James when he said, "Submit yourselves therefore to God. Resist the devil and he will flee from you. Draw near to God and he will draw near to you"(James 4:7–8). I thought, *OK, I think I get the submit myself to God part. How do I resist the devil and draw near to God?* So, in concert with the truth and lie exercise, I wrote a simple prayer that went something like this: "In Jesus name, I reject the lie that I am worthless." This was the resisting the devil part. "In Jesus name, I embrace the truth that You love me, Lord—that You called me into existence for an eternal relationship of love with you. Lord, please heal me and help me escape these lies that lead me to despair. Please take control of my heart and mind." This, of course, was the drawing near to God part.

Over the following months and years, I used that method over and over again to fight against the lies that moved me to anxiety, frustration, and despair, and peace continued to grow in my heart. By God's grace I had experienced great victories with these powerful tools, but He was not finished. His equipping me for the battle continued.

I read another powerful passage that haunted me. The Holy Spirit through Saint Paul in the fourth chapter of his letter to the Philippians said this:

> Rejoice in the Lord always; again I will say, Rejoice.... The Lord is at hand. Have no anxiety about anything, but in everything by prayer and supplication with thanksgiving let your requests be made known to God. And the peace of God, which passes all understanding, will keep your hearts and your minds in Christ Jesus. (Philippians 4:4, 6–7)

I remember reading this passage for the first time. The thing that stuck out to me was that St. Paul said that we should have *no* anxiety about *anything*. My first thought was, *Wow, he's crazy. How can those who were being persecuted, beaten, dying, losing all they had in the persecution of the early Church be told, "have no anxiety about anything"? Is this really possible?* The Holy Spirit reminded me of a passage in the Acts of the Apostles that I had also marveled over: "And when they had called in the apostles, they beat them and charged them not to speak in the name of Jesus, and let them go. Then they left the presence of the council, rejoicing that they were counted worthy to suffer dishonor for the name" (Acts 5:40–42). They were beaten, imprisoned, robbed of their rights, and threatened, yet they "rejoiced." How was this possible? St. James also said, "Count it all joy, my brethren, when you meet various trials" (James 1:2). The word *count* can be translated "consider." Another affirmation of the battle in the mind.

It seemed to me that if I believed the Scriptures and the experience of these men, if I really could take every thought captive, I would be so resilient that nothing in life, not even the worst of circumstances, could rob me of joy and peace! This was so radical a notion to me that I thought it had to be true and inspired by God. It is militantly contrary to the mind of the world. No sane person would ever dare make these claims unless they had experienced it themselves and were inspired by God.

This passage from Philippians contains another powerful weapon in the battle for peace: prayer. The Holy Spirit here tells us to pray and offer our requests and thanksgiving to God so that the peace of God will guard our hearts and minds in Jesus. This was a bit troubling to me because as it is written, one can expect to just pray and peace would then always and easily come. I certainly didn't experience this at the outset. Yes, I experienced an increase in peace, but sometimes the battle was so intense that it took days, weeks, months, and even years to overcome. Even so, He did work this miracle in me — one molecule of my mind and heart at a time, one thought captive at a time, one lie redeemed and replaced by the truth at a time. Some of the battles had to be fought over and over and over again until the lie was completely replaced by the truth and never again had power to draw me to anxiety, fear, despair, and narcissism.

We continue to draw from the wisdom of the Holy Spirit out of St. Paul's words in his letter to the Philippians,

> Finally, brethren, whatever is true, whatever is honorable, whatever is just, whatever is pure, whatever is lovely, whatever is gracious, if there is any excellence, if there is anything worthy of praise, think about these things. What

you have learned and received and heard and seen in me, do; and the God of peace will be with you. (Philippians 4:8–9)

We have another weapon in our arsenal: how and where we focus our minds can impact the experienced presence of God with us, and related to that effort, our peace! There is a word in this passage that can easily be overlooked: *think*. This word can be translated "consider" or "ponder." Another translation is "dwell." The very first passage in the Bible I had memorized was "I have hidden Thy word in my heart that I might not sin against Thee" (Psalm 119:11, KJV). (All the first verses I memorized were in the King James Version). This idea of hiding in my heart the good things and dwelling on the good things seemed to be connected.

It was clear to me that I needed to begin to change the way I lived—what I consumed or allowed into my mind and before my eyes. The earliest outcome of this effort was to fill several garbage cans with music cassettes that I listened to that in no way could rise to the level of "whatever is true, whatever is honorable, whatever is just, whatever is pure, whatever is lovely, whatever is gracious, if there is any excellence, if there is anything worthy of praise." Later I tossed my television. This was one of the best decisions of my life. My peace continued to increase.

At this point I had received quite a cadre of weapons from God to fight the battle against anxiety, worry, fear, and despair:
- Awareness of the battle with the devil in my mind
- Comfort of God that the battle can and will be won with His help
- Discovery of an approach of rejecting lies and embracing truth that had a tangible effect
- Prayers of supplication and thanksgiving

• The need to control what I allowed into my mind
• The practice of actually changing what I allowed into my mind and being more purposeful in pursuing only those things that brought goodness and peace
• The discipline of rejoicing at the trials with the recognition that they are allowed by God for our greater good

My healing was well under way. By God's grace, I was simultaneously exploring Catholic mystical tradition as He was leading me toward the Catholic Church. This mystical tradition, along with the sacraments, brought about the final stages of my healing and the normative reality of peace in the midst of the storm.

Questions for Reflection

• What lies do you believe that drive you to negative thoughts or anxiety?
• Do you allow media and other content into your mind that fails to rise to the standard the Holy Spirit provided through St. Paul in Philippians 4:4–9?
• How often do you deal with negative thoughts? What is the impact on your life? Do you lose sleep? Are relationships often harmed because of your anxiety or frustration?
• How do you feel when you hear Jesus' promise that He gives you peace? Do you feel that peace?

Foundations for Discernment and Navigating the Path of Peace

For those who live according to the flesh set their minds on the things of the flesh, but those who live according to the Spirit set their minds on the things of the Spirit. To set the mind on the flesh is death, but to set the mind on the Spirit is life and peace.

—Romans 8:5–6

I have struggled many times with aridity in prayer. I didn't even know the term *aridity* until I stumbled across it in Catholic mystical tradition and my eyes were opened to this common spiritual challenge. When I became Catholic, I experienced a rapid healing—in particular through the writings of St. Teresa of Avila and a Jesuit priest, Jean-Pierre de Caussade. In Teresa I found a kindred soul—one that understood what a real relationship with Jesus looked like. In de Caussade I found a way to see a vision of God in all things, in every moment. These writers helped to reinforce my commitment to prayer and to filling my mind with truth. I read every translation of de Caussade's works. I read my favorite translation at least five times. The power of his wisdom is in the recognition of the work of God in every moment and every circumstance of life. This helped me to better see God and yield to Him as I experienced circumstances and situations that brought fear, anxiety, and despair to the surface — to be healed.

Next I encountered the wisdom of St. Ignatius of Loyola through the indispensable writings and reflections of Fr. Timothy Gallagher, O.M.V. This was the beginning of the end of the final strongholds that seemed to be too strong to be overcome. My aim for the remainder of this book is to move from my personal story into what I would call a simplified understanding of the practice of discernment of spirits. Before I do so, some important foundational truths must be understood, though I will only explore them in cursory form. They are what I would call a Paradigm of Ascent™ and are the necessary foundations of discernment and the path of healing and peace that God has provided for all of us. These truths are foundational in that if they are not all present in some substantive way, the practice of discernment of spirits is impossible to follow and the promise of peace is impossible to experience.

The first foundational truth is that we must have an authentic "yes" in our heart to God to begin and complete the journey of healing in heaven. It is not enough to merely know about God or even to practice our faith — we must know him intimately. This is the path of the mystics, but it is also the path to heaven. It is a path that everyone can know and must embrace to get to heaven. This path is often obscure to most Catholics because it is not common for someone already in the Church to hear a call to conversion. However, this call to conversion and even the warnings of hell were offered frequently by Jesus to those who were His close followers.[3] Though we have been baptized and confirmed, we still must constantly recognize our need for God and for the conversion of life that draws us ever more closely to

---

[3]   See Matthew 7 as an example.

Him. The Second Vatican Council issued a stern and stunning warning to those who are in the Church but have yet to really embrace the reality of what it means to have a relationship with God and truly live that relationship from the heart:

> They are fully incorporated in the society of the Church who, possessing the Spirit of Christ accept her entire system and all the means of salvation given to her, and are united with her as part of her visible bodily structure and through her with Christ, who rules her through the Supreme Pontiff and the bishops. The bonds which bind men to the Church in a visible way are profession of faith, the sacraments, and ecclesiastical government and communion. He is not saved, however, who, though part of the body of the Church, does not persevere in charity. He remains indeed in the bosom of the Church, but, as it were, only in a "bodily" manner and not "in his heart." All the Church's children should remember that their exalted status is to be attributed not to their own merits but to the special grace of Christ. If they fail moreover to respond to that grace in thought, word and deed, not only shall they not be saved but they will be the more severely judged.[4]

The second foundational element is the most important support for our "yes" of the heart, and it consists of two of the sacraments, the Eucharist and regular confession. It is a mortal sin to miss Mass on Sunday, but beyond the threat of hell, the Eucharist is the most powerful sustenance of our faith, and we should pursue participation in the Holy Sacrifice of the Mass as frequently as possible. The Sacrament of Penance and Reconciliation is also

---

[4]   *Lumen Gentium*, "Dogmatic Constitution on the Church," 14.

absolutely necessary to support our "yes." Too often we underestimate the power of this sacrament. We might think of it merely as a remedy for sin, which is vital and true, but it is also a great grace to strengthen us against falling into sin. Said another way, the Sacrament of Penance both provides forgiveness of sins and strengthens us in our efforts to fight sin. Regardless of either emphasis, if we are not reconciled to God and not living in a state of grace, we are cut off from the life of grace and will not be able to properly discern the difference between the inspirations and influence of God and the temptations and false lies of the devil.

Because of the poor catechesis of our time, I must be clear. Living in a state of grace means that we are living without having unconfessed mortal sins, and we are following the teachings of the Church. To learn more about this, the *Catechism of the Catholic Church* is very clear on these matters and should be studied by every serious Catholic.

The third foundational element to authentic and effective discernment is daily prayer. The most powerful daily prayers are twofold: mental prayer and the Rosary. Sts. Teresa of Avila and Alphonsus Liguori, both Doctors of the Church, consider daily mental prayer as necessary for salvation because of the impact on the soul of those who daily draw near to their Savior in dedicated intimacy. A sound and very practical understanding of the practice of daily mental prayer can be found in my book *Into the Deep: Finding Peace through Prayer*.[5] The Rosary, as revealed by our Blessed Mother, is necessary both for our salvation and that of the world. Together, these two daily prayers provide both protection and a kind of shield and nurturing to our "yes" that allow us to move forward in faith. Whether you have yet to take

---

[5]   Beacon Publishing, 2016.

up the practice of the Rosary or you are a long-time practitioner and need to go deeper or break the pattern of familiarity, I have co-authored a book with Connie Rossini entitled *Contemplative Rosary* that you will find helpful.

The fourth foundational element to our discernment is *ascesis*. This ancient Greek word simply means "exercise." In our usage, that exercise is to exert conscious daily and deliberate effort away from sin and selfishness and toward self-giving to God and our neighbor. It is the practical result of what Jesus meant when he said, "If any man would come after me, let him deny himself and take up his cross and follow me" (Matthew 16:24). Ascesis is simply self-giving and self-denial — saying "no" to the draws of our lower nature in order to say "yes" to giving ourselves completely to God and to those whom He has placed in our care or circle of influence. Ascesis is simply what it means to truly follow Jesus.

This final element completes what I like to call a "saint-making machine." These basic elements are in place in the life of every saint and everyone who makes progress in the spiritual life toward God and peace and away from sin and the sorrows of sin. This Paradigm of Ascent™ is also the necessary basis for beginning to distinguish between the voice and influence of God and the voice and influence of the enemy of our souls.

As we begin to implement these practices, we will lay a foundation that is, in and of itself, the most powerful healing force we can know. We will begin living by what is known in Catholic Tradition as a "rule of life" or what we call in our community a "plan of love."[6] A plan of love is simply a set of concrete commitments

---

[6] I belong to Apostoli Viae, a private association of the faithful dedicated to helping its members and the Church to understand

that we make to God on a daily, weekly, or monthly basis. A simple plan of love might look something like this:

- Daily Mental Prayer—Wake up at 6:00 a.m. and pray for ten minutes, focusing on the Gospel Reading of the day.
- Daily Rosary—Pray one decade in the car on the way to work.
- Attend Mass every Sunday without fail.
- Go to confession every other week.

The final step in our foundation is what is known as an examen prayer, or an examination of conscience. You might have heard the phrase in business: "What gets measured gets done." The same principle applies in the life of someone who truly desires to give themselves to God and to know the peace and joy He has for them. It is common to hear folks shy away from the examen because they have been taught a predominantly negative approach that is solely focused on where they have failed or what they have done wrong. This is not the approach that I recommend. Instead, I encourage practicing the examen in a way that is focused on God's redemptive power and mercy, not our weakness. As St. Paul recalled, "He said to me, 'My grace is sufficient for you, for my power is made perfect in weakness' ... for when I am weak, then I am strong."

The approach I recommend looks something like this. At the same time every night before going to bed, take five minutes to review your day. Then step into your "mental helicopter," fly up about twenty feet and then back to when you got out of bed in the morning. Then slowly fly over your day from morning to evening, asking two simple questions:

---

how to live the contemplative life through authentic Catholic mystical tradition. You can find out more at ApostoliViae.org.

1. *What have I been able to do, by the grace of God, that is honoring to Him and others?* When you discover these things, express praise to God. This can be as simple as "Thank you, Lord, for the ability to pray according to my plan of love when I didn't feel like doing so."
2. *How have I failed to honor God and others in my life?* When you discover these things, you still pray in thanksgiving something like this: "Thank you, Lord, for revealing my sin to me so that I can be forgiven and strengthened to overcome this sin in the future."

Now, this may seem very simple—and it is. However, don't be fooled. This powerful practice is no less important than a compass to someone seeking to find their way through the wilderness. It keeps us awake to our progress on the narrow way to heaven, and it helps ensure that we stay on the path. As you will see in the next chapter, staying awake is critical to hearing and heeding the voice of God and avoiding the influence of the enemy of our souls.

Questions for Reflection

- Which of these foundational spiritual practices do you already have in place and practice as a habit—that is, you do them about 90 percent of the time (or nine out of every ten days)?
- Which of these practices do you not yet have in place?
- What steps can you take to begin to fill in the gaps or make improvements?
- What is a good plan of love for you to start with that is reasonable and measurable?

The Voice of the Devil—The Voice of God

*May the God of hope fill you with all joy and peace in believing,
so that by the power of the Holy Spirit you may abound in hope.*

—Romans 15:13

St. Ignatius was a bad man before his conversion. It is said of him
that he probably had broken every commandment by the time
a cannonball ripped through his leg in a battle he initiated in
his native Spain. During his convalescence, the Lord opened his
eyes to the reality of the spiritual battle around and within him.
His sister-in-law gave him books about the saints, and he had no
better way to pass the time than to read and think. Bedridden
during his long recovery (without a TV, YouTube, or Facebook to
drown out the voice of God), he discovered that when he would
fantasize about worldly conquests and adventures, he would begin
to feel desolate. In contrast, when he considered what it might
be like to become a saint, he was drawn to consolation. This was
the beginning of the remarkable, life-changing wisdom that St.
Ignatius has given the Church, known as discernment of spirits.

Ultimately his wisdom blossomed into a very clear set of
guidelines to help us understand how the devil works—how he
seeks to influence us to hell and anxiety and how God works and

seeks to draw us to heaven and peace. He called these guidelines "Rules" for discernment. The understanding and application of these rules have aided many to become saints.

Years ago, I began to teach a course at the Avila Institute called "Discernment of Spirits 101." What surprised me most about the course was its impact on the students. These students included hundreds of laity, deacons, priests, and religious. I knew that these rules were powerful because of how they changed my life. What I didn't expect was that when others applied the same wisdom, almost universally they would report that they too had experienced what they would categorize as a total spiritual transformation. In fact, on average, over 70 percent of my students reported this level of impact! What follows is an outline and a kind of field guide to these powerful guidelines that, when practiced, will do the same for you.

What Is Discernment?

To discern is to understand and decide on a course of action regarding inspirations that influence our thoughts, words, and deeds either toward God to heaven or away from Him to hell.

In the New Testament and the lives of the saints we have clear examples of the need to test every spirit and determine if they are from God or represent God's will or from the enemy of souls and represent his desires. St. John in his first epistle said, "Beloved, do not believe every spirit, but test the spirits to see whether they are of God (1 John 4:1). St. Paul warned of the same need in his first letter to the Thessalonians where he admonished the Church to "test everything; hold fast what is good" (1 Thessalonians 5:21). Finally, in 1 Corinthians 12, we have the discernment of spirits listed as a gift of the Holy Spirit.

Clearly this is something that the Holy Spirit desires that we pursue with all diligence in order to understand the forces that seek to influence us, human, divine, and demonic. Now let's turn our attention to understanding the basics about the sources of inspirations and then the process of discernment.

Where Do the Inspirations Come From?

Inspirations have three sources:

1. *The "Good Spirits"*: These good spirits cause *consolation* and seek to lead us to God, to the Good, to selflessness, to union with God, and ultimately to heaven. These spirits are dispatched by God and only seek our good.
2. *The "Bad Spirits"*: The bad spirits cause *desolation* and lead us to the world, the flesh, the devil, selfishness, and ultimately hell. These spirits only seek to do us harm.
3. *You*: Your sensual appetites, sickness, addictions, beliefs, desires, strengths, weaknesses, and diseases due to original sin can cause many kinds of non-spiritual consolation and desolation, and your own makeup can also amplify spiritual consolation and desolation.

What Is the Process for Exercising Discernment of Spirits?

The process of discernment has three steps:

1. *To Be Aware*: We are aware of ourselves—whether or not we are in consolation or desolation; we recognize the forces that are at play on a daily basis for and against our holiness, our peace, and our progress to God.

2. *To Understand:* We accurately interpret the forces at play on us or in us.
3. *To Take Action:* We take appropriate action depending on the movements of these spirits.
   A. *Bad Spirits — Resist:* We resist the movements of the bad spirits.
   B. *Good Spirits — Embrace:* We embrace the movements of the good spirits.

At this point you might ask, "Wait, what are the definitions of consolation and desolation? How do we know if we are in one or the other and how do we know what to do?" St. Ignatius provides us with these definitions and even lists examples in the fourteen rules of discernment that he developed. Next we'll focus on the specific rules St. Ignatius laid out to help us know what is going on and what to do about it. As we explore and practice these rules, the process we just outlined above will become clearer.

Rules for Discernment of Spirits

Rule #1: For Those Moving from Mortal Sin to Mortal Sin

> In the persons who go from mortal sin to mortal sin, the enemy will propose apparent pleasures, making them imagine sensual delights and pleasures in order to enslave them more and make them grow in their vices and sins. In these persons the good spirit uses a contrary method, pricking them and disturbing their consciences through the process of reason and moral judgment.

This first rule is simple and straightforward because it only applies to a specific state of soul that the rest of the thirteen rules do not. St. Ignatius reveals that this rule is for someone who is stuck in a cycle of moving from mortal sin to mortal sin. Said another way, this person regularly and habitually chooses to commit the same or many mortal sins over and over again and has yet to begin to fight against this life pattern. In this case, here's how the good and bad spirits work:

Bad Spirits: Will propose apparent pleasures, making the person imagine sensual delights and pleasures in order to enslave them more and make them grow in their vices and sins.

Good Spirits: Will prick the person's conscience through the process of reason and moral judgment.

Let's take a very common example of this situation in which the worst kind of advice is often heard: A man and woman are living together, or are sexually involved together, outside of marriage. In this case, it is safe to assume that both persons are living in habitual mortal sin because sexual activity is reserved for marriage, and its practice outside of marriage is always a mortal sin.

How does the good spirit act in this case? The good spirit robs both of them of peace! To *prick* is to cause mental or emotional discomfort. The good spirit might say something like this to the man in this situation: "This woman is a child of God. You have robbed her of her innocence, and you continue to cause her to sin by allowing this relationship to continue." The goal of the good spirit is to convict this man of sin and thereby help him to choose to break this pattern of sin by either ending the relationship or ending the sinful behavior.

How will the bad spirit act? The bad spirit will remind the man that he loves and desires the woman and that she loves and desires him. In particular, the bad spirit will point out how good they feel when they are together. The bad spirit will whisper in both of their ears, "You both love one another; how could this possibly be wrong?"

What is fascinating about this situation is that the most common advice given to folks attempting to discern what to do in a situation like this is to follow where peace leads—follow your heart. In this case, the bad spirit is the one giving a kind of pseudo-peace by reminding the couple how good they feel when they are together. We can rightly argue that this peace is not authentic peace, but it doesn't matter. What matters is that if peace is the measure chosen and the bad spirit produces something that feels like "peace," then the advice given would be deeply harmful to this couple.

In contrast, the good spirit has actually caused the opposite of peace and seeks to create inner turmoil. "Peace" in this case is not the measure of how to discern. The fact is that when one is in habitual mortal sin, we need to embrace the good spirit and listen to the arguments of how this or that act is immoral and damaging. We need to embrace the sorrow of the situation and allow it to turn us to repentance and seek to exit as quickly and decisively as we can. This cleansing sorrow, though it is hard to understand, is actually a kind of consolation. In the next rule we will explore this a bit further.

Finally, it is important to note that St. Ignatius not only wrote rules of discernment; he also wrote rules for thinking *with* the Church. Suffice it to say that if we ever have "peace" about something that leads us away from the Church or to some belief or action that is contrary to the magisterium and Tradition, this "peace" is a false peace from the bad spirit and contrary to the will of God.

Questions for Reflection

• Have you ever experienced the bad advice to "follow your heart?" What was the result?

• Do you struggle with habitual sin? If so, are you aware that you can be totally free of this habitual sin through the sacraments of the Church and your cooperation with God?

• What steps can you take to begin to fight more diligently against mortal sin or any habitual sin in your life?[7]

---

[7] You will find a number of helpful resources for this battle against habitual sin in the Recommended Resources section of this book.

Rule #2: For Those Moving from Good to Better

> In persons who are going on intensely cleansing their sins and rising from good to better in the service of God our Lord, it is the method contrary to that in the first rule, for then it is the way of the evil spirit to disturb, sadden and put obstacles, disquieting with false reasons, so that the person may be stopped in their progress.... It is proper to the good spirit to give courage and strength, consolations, tears, inspirations and quiet, easing, and removing all obstacles, that one may be encouraged in their progress.

First, it is important to note that the player's approach to the game has changed significantly from rule one to rules two to fourteen. From the second to the fourteenth rule, the person we are speaking about is one who is "intensely cleansing their sins and rising from good to better." What does this person look like? We answered that question in detail in the chapter "Foundations for Discernment." If you are pursuing most or all of the foundations of the spiritual life outlined there and no longer giving yourself over to habitual mortal sin without a fight and having some success, then rules two to fourteen apply to you. If you are still unclear of what it means to live free from "habitual" mortal sin, it simply means that the sins you commit are not mortal and the sins you do commit are not the same sins committed over and over. If you are unclear about the distinction between mortal and venial sin, now is probably a good time to set this book down, grab your *Catechism*, and read paragraphs 1846 to 1876. You might be surprised—hopefully in a good way.

OK, so how do the good spirits and bad spirits work in persons going from good to better with respect to rule number two?

Bad Spirits: Will provide inspirations to sadness; will draw you to focus on obstacles (potential or real) in order *to keep you from making spiritual progress.*

Good Spirits: Will provide courage and strength, consolations, tears, inspirations and quiet, easing and removing all obstacles *in order that you may be encouraged in your progress.*

To illustrate this, I will share a situation I experienced one recent Lenten season. I had determined to give up eating breakfast and was fasting daily. (Don't worry—this is not boasting. I really need no more than two medium-size meals each day to stay at a healthy weight.) So basically I was just fasting to fight the gluttony that set in as my metabolism slowed down. One day near the end of Lent, as I came out of daily Mass, I had the thought to get my favorite fast-food breakfast at Chick-fil-A. I was hungry, and I was drawn more deeply into that hunger the moment I noticed it. I thought, *No, I am not going to do that.* And then I found myself almost involuntarily taking a right turn toward Chick-fil-A rather than turning left toward home. The arguments came: "You are hungry. Look, you have done a great job this Lent. Besides, the doc says your weight is fine. What's the downside? It will taste fantastic." Next, however, I heard a peaceful reassurance: "Lent is almost over. You can handle one more day. It's time to go home." By God's grace, I turned my truck around and went home. The consolations were strong and clear, and I was grateful and encouraged. It also dawned on me that I had just lived through a good and somewhat humorous rule-two scenario that I could share with my students.

Of course, there are many more grave matters that can play out in this rule than whether or not to have a breakfast burrito. I have had priests and deacons tell me that as they were heading to their ordination, they heard powerful, almost paralyzing voices telling them that they were not worthy. I have had good laypeople who were beginning a new ministry in their parish or college group tell me that they, too, had strong arguments in their heads about their unworthiness, about how busy they were, and how they were overdoing it. The bad spirits are always ready to give you false reasons why you can't or shouldn't do the thing God is asking you to do.

Now, this might prompt you to ask the question: "Can the devil put thoughts into my mind?" St. Teresa of Avila, in her book *Interior Castle*, reveals the answer:

> For God does not deny Himself to anyone who perseveres. Little by little He will measure out the courage sufficient to attain this victory. I say "courage" because there are so many things *the devil puts in the minds of beginners to prevent them from starting out on this path.* For the devil knows the damage that will be done him in losing not only that one

soul but many others. . . . The devil puts so many dangers
and difficulties into the beginner's head that no little
courage, but a great deal, is necessary in order not to turn
back — and a great deal of assistance from God.[8]

It is generally understood that demons can put thoughts in our
heads and make suggestions to us. This basic assumption is foundational to St. Ignatius's understanding of how desolation and
related temptations to sin come about.

One of the things I tell my students is: "All the thoughts
in your head are not yours, and you shouldn't listen to them."
The beginning of learning to understand the influence of the
enemy in our hearts and minds is realizing how common and
normative it is that the enemy works to influence us through
our thoughts. This strategy is particularly powerful when he
proposes ideas connected to past wounds. This was a big part
of why my own healing took so long. By God's grace, when we
begin to see these efforts on the part of the enemy for what they
are, we recognize that we can overcome them both by fighting
them in the moment and by pursuing deeper healing regarding
past wounds. So, present anxiety is often an invitation of God
to the healing of past wounds.

Questions for Reflection

• Have you ever experienced something that seemed to be
a temptation or evil suggestion that came from outside
of you?

---

[8]   St. Teresa of Avila, *Interior Castle*, *Life* 11:4 (ICS translation),
emphasis added.

Rule #2: For Those Moving from Good to Better

- How does the idea that all the thoughts in your head are not yours strike you?
- Are you moving from good to better or do you need to make some life changes? If you do need to make changes, what are they? What is your specific plan to do so?

Rule #3: What Is Consolation Exactly?

I call it consolation when some interior movement is caused in the soul, through which the soul becomes inflamed with love of its Creator and Lord, and consequently when it can love no other created thing on the face of the earth in itself, but only in the Creator of them all. Likewise, when the soul sheds tears that move to love of its Lord, whether out of sorrow for one's sins, or for the passion of Christ our Lord, or because of other things directly ordered to his service and praise.

Finally, I call consolation every increase of hope, faith, and charity, with all interior joy that calls and attracts to heavenly things and to the salvation of one's soul, quieting it and giving it peace in its Creator and Lord.

Consolation: An interior movement to God, toward faith, hope, and love, that is caused by the good spirits.

When in Consolation, I May Experience:
- An increase of hope, or faith, or love, or all three
- My heart inflamed with love of God and goodness

Spiritual Warfare and the Discernment of Spirits

- Shedding of tears for love of God, sorrow for my sin, or gratitude
- Experiences of interior joy
- A clear draw to heavenly things
- Quiet and peace in the Lord

No matter how consolation specifically surfaces within us, if it is authentic, it will always draw us to submit to the magisterium of the Church and to God's will and ways. It is really no more complicated than that. The challenge is that if we are not well catechized—and most of us are not—we may not understand or even notice when we are led astray. By God's grace we have a catechism that addresses all the most important topics of our faith. The more we know our faith, the better our practice of discernment will be.

As you review the list of the experiences of consolation above, you might ask: "How can I experience consolation, which seems like it would be a good feeling, but also sorrow for sin, which it seems rational to experience as a bad feeling?" I'll share two personal examples. Before I became Catholic, I used to mock the teachings of the Catholic Church. One of the teachings I aggressively mocked was the role of the Blessed Mother. I was relentlessly negative about any thought that Mary was special in any way other than that she made a good decision to say "yes" to God. One weekday after I converted to Catholicism, I attended daily Mass. It was the Feast of Our Lady of Sorrows. That day I saw a beautiful icon depicting her suffering by the seven swords in her heart. It touched me that she looked so sad. During Mass I was struck with my sinful treatment of Mary, and I then became overwhelmed with sorrow and my tears flowed. I asked God and the Blessed Mother for forgiveness, and I felt a powerful consolation and spiritual cleansing. It wasn't joyful, but it was good.

Recently, at the death of my father, my middle brother, David, and I reconciled. This experience was similarly bittersweet. I was deeply saddened that we had lost so many years and even more grateful that we are now back together as a family. Even though these experiences brought me a revelation of the gravity of sin, I simultaneously knew that God had healed and forgiven me and then restored more than I ever lost. This is just one way that sorrow for sin can actually be a consolation.

Questions for Reflection

• How is your daily examen going? Are you beginning to notice your interior inclinations and their sources? Are you focusing on the positive work of God and His redemptive grace in your life? If you are struggling to keep this commitment, is there someone who can help you to be accountable? What is your next step to put that accountability into place?

• Have you ever experienced any of the experiences of consolation that St. Ignatius speaks about?

• What did that consolation lead you to do? How did it affect you?

Rule #4: What Exactly Is Desolation?

I call desolation all the contrary of the third rule, such as darkness of soul, disturbance in it, movement to low and earthly things, disquiet from various agitations and temptations, moving to lack of confidence, hopelessness, finding oneself totally slothful, tepid, sad, and as if separated from one's Creator and Lord.

For just as consolation is contrary to desolation, in the same way the thoughts that come from consolation are contrary to the thoughts that come from desolation.

Desolation: Any movement toward our lower nature and inclinations toward doubt, despair, or narcissism caused by the bad spirits.

When in Desolation, I Might Experience:
- Movement to doubt, or despair, or narcissism or some combination of all three
- Movement to low and earthly things — the draws of our lower nature and our senses
- A decrease in love of God or heavenly things
- Darkness of soul and disturbance

- A disquiet with agitations and temptations
- A lack of confidence, or hope, or love, or any combination of all three
- A feeling of being lazy, tepid, or sad, or as if separated from God

For someone just beginning to explore this spiritual discipline, desolation is actually an easier experience to identify than consolation. The challenge is that when we are in desolation, if we are just at the beginning of our journey of learning to fight it, it can be a debilitating feeling. Even if we recognize what is happening, it won't seem as if we can do anything about it. The experience can be so powerful that it feels as though we can't escape, we can't fight, or we can't make the decision we know is right in spite of our knowledge or desire. It is as if we have had a spell cast over us or as if we have woken up on the wrong side of the bed and all is dark and repulsive to us and we can't conceive of snapping out of it.

By God's grace, it is often true that the moment we make a decision to fight this desolation, we allow God to begin to give us His strength and ability to break out of the darkness. On a number of occasions while in desolation, I have had no sense that I had the strength to resist it. Still, as an act of faith, I made the slightest movement to fight it with nothing but faint confidence in God's desire that I fight. In that moment, I experienced a surge of strength from God and was able to break free of the pull of desolation. This has not been an uncommon experience, nor is it one unique to me.

A common tactic of the enemy with respect to desolation is to try to draw us out of the present moment, where we are and where God is, into the future or the past in order to disable or discourage us in our holy or healthy aspirations. The evil one does this in two ways, depending upon our makeup, tendencies, strengths, and weaknesses. If you are a past-oriented person, the tactic will often be to remind you of your past sins, weaknesses, and failures in order to convince you that you can't possibly move forward with your plans to honor God or do some good. If you are a future-oriented person or someone prone to worry about the future, you will likely face visions of failure and scenarios that seek to persuade you that you are not able to move forward with your project and that you should abandon it. Here are some of the temptations reported by my students as we reflected on these tactics:

- I am particularly prone to spiritual desolation just prior to meeting with supplicants in our healing ministry. I start to think that I am perhaps not well-enough equipped to work with people or I start to experience foggy thinking, and so I find excuses not to meet or I postpone to a later date.

- As I reflect on my times of desolation, I realize one of two things. Either I am self-absorbed, or I am dwelling on something in my past or in the future. Sometimes both!

- What I experience in desolation very frequently are thoughts that any prior sense of growth in and attestations of love for God, longing for the things of God, affection, fervor, good intentions, and resolutions were all disingenuous.

A powerful practice and perspective to combat these tactics is to be aware and to use your practice of the examen to reveal when you are tempted to leave the present moment and move into the past or the future. When this happens, it is time to stop, focus on what is happening in your mind, and renounce these temptations in the name of Jesus. You can then practice the "lie juxtaposed with the truth exercise" in the "Invitation to Healing" chapter. One important note with this tool is that writing it out is vital in order to get the thoughts out of your head onto paper. Negative thoughts have much more power when they are hidden in our heads instead of brought out to the light of day where we can objectively consider them.

Questions for Reflection

- Are you a past-oriented or future-oriented person?
- How has the enemy caused you desolation with respect to the past? What has caused you anxiety or suffering in the past?
- How has the enemy caused you desolation with respect to the future? What causes anxiety or suffering with respect to possibilities in the future?
- What are the most common lies you tend to believe or be easily drawn into?
- What are the corresponding truths that, if you believed them, would set you free to do God's will?

Rule #5: What Is the Most Important Decision I Can Make When in Desolation?

In times of desolation never make a change, but be firm and constant in the proposals and determinations in which one was the day preceding such desolation, or in the determination in which one was in the preceding consolation.

Because, as in consolation the good spirit guides and counsels us more, so in desolation the bad spirit, with whose counsels we cannot find the way to a right decision.

Rule #5 (in a Nutshell): When in desolation, don't change commitments made while in consolation.

For simplicity's sake, let's break this down with an example:

Day One: You attend a conference on mental prayer and are greatly encouraged (consolation) and decide to begin practicing this prayer on a daily basis. You make a commitment to get up thirty minutes earlier to read the Scriptures and reflect on them in the presence of

God. The more you think about it, the more you are encouraged.

Day Two: After a restless night due to a nightmare and worry about things at work, your alarm goes off. You wake up feeling very sluggish and discouraged and a negative suggestion emerges (desolation). "You are tired and have lots to do today at work. You really should take care of yourself and go back to sleep." The voice continues, "You know, you always bite off more than you can chew" (an echo of a distant parental criticism). You begin to feel worse.

Now well practiced in discernment, you remember that you need to stop when you feel desolation, and so you do. You sit up in bed and ask yourself, "Have I really bitten off more than I can chew?" You notice that you are feeling dark and realize that you are in desolation. What should you do? How do you apply rule number five? The answer is simple: *don't make a change at this moment;* keep the commitment you made when you were in consolation whether you feel like it or not. When you emerge out of desolation or are in consolation, you can reevaluate. For now, the decision is *no changes*.

In the second half of rule five, St. Ignatius provides important wisdom as to the "why" behind the rule of "no changes when in desolation." You might think the answer is already clear because desolation is from the enemy. Unfortunately, the answer isn't quite that simple as it plays out in day-to-day life. Learning to understand the ebb and flow of consolation and desolation is not a black-and-white science, but rather an intuitive art that improves with attentive and prayerful observation and action.

For instance, with regard to the scenario we just evaluated, what if thirty minutes really isn't wise after all? What if the desolation was against the movement toward God and, at the same time, the decision also wasn't prudent—perhaps you should reduce your first attempts at mental prayer to a more reasonable first step of just ten minutes? What should you do in this case, in the moment? You should follow the rule and change nothing until you return to consolation.

Why is that? Well, when we are in consolation, the voice of the good spirit—how well we can hear and understand these positive inspirations—is very clear. Said another way, in consolation the voice or inspiration of the good spirit is louder and clearer. So, in consolation, it is more likely that we will make good decisions as we seek to respond to God's leading.

In contrast, when we are in desolation, the voice or inspiration of the good spirit is hard to hear and understand. This is something similar to what happens when we are hiking in the woods and fog sets in and we are visually separated from a companion. We can call out, and they can call back, but their voice is so faint that we can't hear them clearly enough to figure out where they are and where we need to go to find them. We must wait until the fog lifts and we can better interpret the terrain and better decipher how we should proceed to clarity. At that point, we shout out to our lost friend, "Don't move! The sun is coming up. Let's wait until the fog lifts!"

If there is no other rule that you remember in this first encounter with the rules of discernment, remember rule number five. Follow it, and you will never regret it, and if you are like me, it will demonstrate the power of the rules and help to bring you back to them if they happen to fade in your focus.

Questions for Reflection

- Have you ever made a decision in the past where you violated rule number five? What important decision did you make when you were in distress? What was the outcome?
- Have you ever, without knowing the rules, kept rule number five? What was the outcome?
- Have you experienced a time of desolation when you weren't able to think clearly and then, after a time, clarity returned?
- How are you doing with your examen prayer? Do you need to work harder to establish an accountability partner?

Rule #6: What Changes Should I Make When in Desolation?

> Although in desolation we should not change our first proposals (rule five), it is very advantageous to change ourselves intensely against the desolation itself, by insisting *more* upon prayer, meditation, upon much examination, and upon extending ourselves in some suitable way of doing penance.

Here's a breakdown of this simple rule: When desolation sets in, we must redouble our efforts to do what we committed to when in consolation. We do this by:

• Changing ourselves intensely against the desolation
• Insisting on more prayer and meditation
• Pursuing much examination
• Doing penance

St. Ignatius can be confusing here if we move too fast. First he says don't make a change; then he says make a change. However, his first principle to not make a change is in relationship to reducing or setting aside the spiritual commitments we made while in consolation. Here in rule number six he is saying to make a change but in the opposite direction as proposed by the desolation. Rather than turning down or reducing our commitment, we need to turn it up!

How would this look in the previous example about your commitment to prayer? You made a commitment to practice mental prayer for a half-hour; instead of fulfilling that commitment exactly, you would choose to pray for thirty-one minutes rather than thirty. Yes, just one minute more, which is 101 percent more activity than the bad spirit was seeking to tempt you to do.

Why is this important? Does it really help? To answer the last question first, it absolutely does help. The reason is found in St. James's letter to the Church (that means you): "Submit yourselves therefore to God. Resist the devil and he will flee from you. Draw near to God and he will draw near to you" (James 4:7–8). God promises that if we resist the devil, the devil will flee from us. James ties this resistance to the importance of drawing near to God. This is kind of like facing down the skinny, four-foot-tall bully with a hundred-foot-tall muscle man standing behind us. No chance the bully is going to advance toward us in this situation. Pride may cause the enemy to think about it for a moment, but there is no doubt that he will eventually back down. This passage in St. James is the best summary of the rules of discernment found in Scripture.

There is more to explore in the wisdom of this rule. We have covered the first step in changing ourselves by moving against the desolation part. This is the most foundational application of the rule, but there is more.

The next thing we need to do is take a moment to pray and ask, "Why am I experiencing this desolation?" This question and the corresponding action falls under the Ignatian admonition to practice "meditation" and "much examination." We do this to gain understanding and perspective regarding possible underlying causes and to become more aware of all that is at play in the situation (e.g., the bad spirits, our weaknesses, etc.).

I write this after having just arrived in Rome the day before. I was already tired from travel and had physical difficulties on the plane (due to a lifelong illness issue). I was very uncomfortable, had difficulty breathing, and couldn't sleep. We landed in the early morning, and I was feeling off. I was in physical desolation due to my health and lack of sleep, and emotional and borderline spiritual desolation because of frustration with a situation brewing in Rome that impacted me personally. The more I thought about it, the more desolate I became. All the while I was aware of my struggle, and I discussed it with my wife (rule number thirteen, but that comes later). We determined that we should spend time in prayer and away from work in order to reset after a good night of sleep. We did, and the next day I had sufficient resilience to hit the issues head on in Rome, and all turned out well.

The final step is that St. Ignatius asks us to do some kind of penance. Simply resisting the desolation can fall into the same category as praying longer and practicing some kind of sacrifice with the intention of strengthening our will and honoring God in the decisions we make. This need not be complicated—just a simple act of self-sacrifice for the sake of turning our heart, mind, and will in submission to God's greater purposes.

Questions for Reflection

• Have you ever faced your desolation and refused to give in to it? How did God's grace manifest in that situation?

Spiritual Warfare and the Discernment of Spirits

- Have you ever faced desolation and failed to fight it? What happened?
- Does it make sense that God's voice is hard to hear and the devil's voice is loud when you are in desolation?

Rule #7: How Can I Adjust My Thinking While in Desolation in Order to Better Overcome It?

> Let the one in desolation consider how the Lord has left him in trial in his natural powers, so that he may resist the various agitations and temptations of the enemy; since he can resist with the divine help, which always remains with him, though he does not clearly feel it. . . .
>
> For the Lord has taken away from him his great fervor, abundant love, and intense grace, leaving him, however, sufficient grace for eternal salvation.

Taking every thought captive to God is a difficult affair when we are in desolation. This is because the voice of God is faint and so is the positive experience of the presence of God. St. Ignatius notes that in desolation we have no fervor; our motivation is diminished. Still, he asserts, we do have sufficient grace for eternal salvation. Said another way, our desolation has not diminished the love or grace of God, but only our experience of it. And we have sufficient grace to fight. This is a very important point. Just because we don't feel God's presence, and we do feel the negative forces opposed to our best aspirations, that doesn't mean that God is not present. In fact, His grace and presence may be stronger in this moment than when we feel elated about the person and presence of God.

The year concluding the writing of this book was extremely difficult for me. I lost my father, and I became the president of the largest Catholic news organization in the world. The Vigano letter emerged the same day I was appointed president. The spiritual warfare, personal attacks, and emotional and physical suffering were extreme. I was hospitalized many times during the year because of the resurgence of a lifelong illness. By God's grace, I was blessed with desolation to bring me to the end of myself so that he could further heal and strengthen me. It was clear that He was doing a work in me, and as I sought to understand, He revealed that He allowed me to come to this place so I would cry out to Him for healing and strength. I was weary and at the end of myself, and this, by God's love, was exactly where He needed me to be so that I would yield more fully to His will and ways in my life.

St. Ignatius beckons us, in the entirety of the discipline and practice of discernment, to lift our hearts and minds to what God is actually doing in the moment. He invites us to explore how God is using the circumstances and internal realities of desolation in order that we might strengthen our will against the forces within and outside of us that draw us away from the will and presence of God. In this case, St. Ignatius is asking us to explore what it means to be left alone in our natural powers. Why? The passage from St. James reveals the answer: "God opposes the proud, but gives grace to the humble." As we experience our weakness when God is not empowering us through consolation, we are brought to a place where everything within us that opposes God through pride is militated against, and as our great need is exposed to us, we reach out to Him in humility.

Questions for Reflection

- Is it becoming clearer how we must control our thoughts — to manage what we are thinking and replace the lies with the truth? How does this play out in your life?
- If we cooperate, how does God increase our humility during desolation?
- What is a way we can encourage ourselves during desolation regarding the provision and presence of God in our lives?

Rule #8: How Can I Better Persevere When I Am in Desolation?

> Let one who is in desolation work to be in patience, which is contrary to the vexations which come to him, and let him think that he will soon be consoled, diligently using the means against such desolation, as is said in the sixth rule.

I have had the blessed misfortune of being hospitalized more times than I can count. After a dozen or so near misses with death and loads of pain and suffering, I began to notice a pattern that ultimately became reassuring. I would get sick and feel terrible, I would enter the hospital and get treatment or surgery, which would feel terrible, and then I would get better and go home. There is a lot of gory detail that I will spare you, but after a while, the pattern became reassuring because in every case, I knew that I would heal, and eventually the pain and after-effects of surgery would subside. This awareness and understanding of the normal ebb and flow of sickness and recovery began to help me cope when I was in the midst of suffering. Now, to be clear, I am speaking of physical, not spiritual desolation. Though they can and will often go hand in hand, they are different. That said, the analogy is still important with respect to how we deal with the onslaught of desolation and how we manage our minds in the process.

Similarly, when we are in desolation and just beginning to realize these ebbs and flows, it feels like the desolation will never end. This is part of the lie of the enemy when we are in the midst of it. But when we gain experience through the perspective offered by the Holy Spirit and St. Ignatius, we begin to recognize the pattern when we are in it, and thereby we have hope because we know the desolation will eventually end. This is what St. Ignatius is pointing us to when he says:

- We must fight to be patient as an act of the will no matter how we feel. We must not be timid in this fight but be ruthless against the desolation in the way we manage our thoughts and fight negative thoughts. We must never allow ourselves to sulk or wallow in our misery but affirm the truth of God that we will be freed of this desolation in due time.

- We must tell ourselves the truth that we will emerge out of desolation and that consolation will eventually return. When we do this, we should say it out loud. I have done this in the hospital – "I am going to be fine. This will end. I will feel better in a few days." These affirmations of hope open the door to God's comfort that the future will be a place where there is less pain and suffering even if it is only an ebb in the suffering for a time.

Questions for Reflection

- As a child, were you ever on a car ride with your parents that seemed endless but only seemed that way because you didn't know where you were in the journey?

Rule #8: How Can I Better Persevere?

- Have you ever used this rule without knowing it? What was the situation? How did your awareness of the normal ebb and flow help you?
- Is there a current situation in your life that you are worried will never change? How might choosing patience in the face of your feelings make a difference?

Rule #9: What Are the Causes of Desolation?

There are three principal causes for desolation. The first is because we are tepid, slothful, or negligent in our spiritual exercises, and so through our faults spiritual consolation withdraws from us. The second, to try us and reveal where we really are and how much we extend ourselves in His service and praise without payment of consolations and increased graces. The third, to give us true recognition and understanding so that we may interiorly feel that it is not ours to attain or maintain increased devotion, intense love, tears or any other spiritual consolation, but that all is the gift and grace of God our Lord, and so that we may not build a nest in something belonging to another, raising our mind in some pride or vainglory, attributing to ourselves the devotion or consolation.

As you are hopefully beginning to see, these rules are not discrete and separate from one another. Instead, they overlap and reinforce and build upon one another. Though we have had hints as to the reason God allows desolation, now we have a clear statement of the purpose of God in and through these challenges.

First Reason — To Help Us See
That We Are in Spiritual Danger

Here we return to the analogy of the dashboard lights in a car. The Lord loves us and wants us to recognize when we are too close to the edge of the narrow way and at risk of going over the edge. My wife's new-used car has an excellent feature that detects when the car is drifting and touching one of the lines that demarks lanes or the edge of the road. When the car crosses the edge of one of those lines and the turn signal is not on, it warns the driver with a *Beep! Beep! Beep!* I really hate those beeps, but I have learned to appreciate them, especially when I am driving and tired. In a similar way, the beeps of desolation are there to warn us that we are becoming tepid, slothful, or negligent in our spiritual exercises. In other words, we have become "lukewarm" in our faith or spiritual disciplines.

Believe it or not, being lukewarm is more dangerous to our souls than is crossing the line into headlong traffic. Here's a warning from the Book of Revelation that reveals how truly dangerous this state is:

I know your works: you are neither cold nor hot. Would that you were cold or hot! So, because you are lukewarm, and neither cold nor hot, I will spew you out of my mouth. For you say, I am rich, I have prospered, and I need nothing; not knowing that you are wretched, pitiable, poor, blind, and naked. Therefore I counsel you to buy from me gold refined by fire, that you may be rich, and white garments to clothe you and to keep the shame of your nakedness from being seen, and salve to anoint your eyes, that you may see. Those whom I love, I reprove and chasten; so be zealous and repent. Behold, I stand at the door and knock; if anyone hears my voice and opens the door, I will come in to him and eat with him, and he with me. He who conquers, I will grant him to sit with me on my throne, as I myself conquered and sat down with my Father on his throne. He who has an ear, let him hear what the Spirit says to the churches. (Revelation 3:15–22)

In this passage the Spirit is sending a message to the Church of Laodicea. The passage has a strong warning, but it is also coupled by the message that the warning — and as applies to our course of study, the desolation — is an invitation to healing. This healing is not just a return to our last state before we began to decide to slack off from our spiritual disciplines, but one that results in an even deeper relationship with God if we will pursue a deeper understanding of the challenge and how it has emerged or is rooted in wounds of the past.

Second Reason — To Understand the True State of Our Love of God

Because of concupiscence and the scars left from our sin, we have an infinite capacity for self-deception. When we are asked to evaluate our spiritual state, or other virtues, our tendency is to judge ourselves in light of what we desire to be true rather than what is actually true. On top of that, some of us have a tendency to give ourselves credit just for desiring to be good even if we never act upon it, or even if we act contrary to that desire. Desolation can be a gift of God to help us understand how much we really love Him or how much of our love is immature, narcissistic and purely based on the gifts of consolation.

As a Hebrew Catholic (who was once an unfulfilled Jew), I love the memory of the Passover ceremony where we sing the *Dayeinu*. *Dayeinu* means "it would have been enough" and is a song of praise and thanksgiving written more than a thousand years ago. The following is a beautiful reflection and Christian perspective on what it means to be grateful and to love God for what He has done for us:

Dayeinu—It Would Have Been Enough[9]

If He had rescued us from Egypt,
but not punished the Egyptians,
It would have been enough. (*Dayeinu*)

If He had punished the Egyptians,
but not divided the Red Sea before us,
It would have been enough. (*Dayeinu*)

If He had divided the Red Sea before us,
but not supplied us in the desert for 40 years,
It would have been enough. (*Dayeinu*)

If He had supplied us in the desert for 40 years,
but not brought us to the land of promise,
It would have been enough. (*Dayeinu*)

If He had brought us to the land of promise,
but not made us a holy people,
It would have been enough. (*Dayeinu*)

[9] Inspired by a reflection by Lois Tverberg; https://engediresource-center.com/2015/07/09/dayeinu-it-would-have-been-enough/.

How much more, then, are we to be grateful to God for all of these good things which he has indeed done for all of us!

As Christians who have the fullness of faith, we might also write our *Dayeinu* like this:

> If He had redeemed me with His suffering and
> death,
> but not given me His body and blood in the Eucharist,
> it would have been enough.

> If He had given me His body and blood in the
> Eucharist,
> but not filled me with His Spirit,
> it would have been enough.

> If He had filled me with His Spirit,
> but did not guide my life daily as His disciple,
> it would have been enough.

> If He guided my life daily as His disciple,
> but did not lovingly answer my prayers,
> it would be enough.

> If He lovingly answered my prayers,
> but did not give me His promise to spend eternity
> with Him,
> it would be enough.

How much more, then, are we to be grateful to God for all of these good things which he has indeed done for all of us!

Spiritual Warfare and the Discernment of Spirits

Sometimes we don't appreciate what God has already done for us. We can show our lack of love by expecting constant blessings in order that we might be motivated to serve Him rather than serving Him because He has already done so much and deserves so much more than we could ever give in return. A heart of gratitude is often the antidote to desolation.

Third Reason — To Help Us Know That He Is the Source of All the Good within Us

Catholics sometimes are criticized by Protestants who claim we think we can earn our salvation by our good works. In some sense the criticism is true for many who live their lives by a kind of system whereby we think we are good and thereby worthy of his blessings. Another version is that we act good and thereby deserve His blessings. This mentality can also bleed into a false perception that we are the reason we are able to maintain or cause an increase in our devotion to God. Desolation is the bitter antidote to this dangerous temptation to see ourselves as the captain of our ship and master of our own destiny. In our reflection on the second reasons, we touched on the reality that without Him we are nothing and really deserve nothing. In fact, the only thing any living soul has ever earned on their own is hell. This kind of reflection and corresponding recognition leads us to humility and to cry out to Him as our only true hope and salvation.

Questions for Reflection

• Have you ever taken God's blessings for granted? What were they?

- Would you easily love Him as you do now if He took away all of your material goods?
- If your answer was not an immediate "yes" to question number two, have you ever spent time meditating on Jesus suffering in His passion? If not, now might be a good time to do that. The best way is to use either St. Alphonsus Ligouri's or St. Francis of Assisi's reflections on the stations of the cross because they both help us focus on our part in Christ's suffering and all that He has suffered for us and in our behalf.

Rule #10: How Should I Act or Prepare When I Am in Consolation?

> Let the one who is in consolation think how he will conduct himself in the desolation which will come after, taking new strength for that time.

You might notice again that St. Ignatius's approach to desolation is that he always works to pull us up and out of the feelings of the situation and into a place where we have greater perspective. In this case he clearly indicates that the ebb and flow of consolation and desolation is something that we will face for the entirety of our lives. As well, he wants us to know that when we are in consolation, desolation will follow and that there is benefit in preparing for it.

Some people live with a constantly disordered perspective of the future as if it will always be rosy or that life will, in general, be easy at some point. Yes, life may be better at some point. For me, my health has become more under control in my forties and beyond and my married life has improved dramatically. God has brought about a great deal of healing physically, spiritually, and emotionally in this latter stage of my life. However, that doesn't mean that I still won't be brought to the end of myself through desolation or even other acts or allowances of God that help to reveal the need for more healing and more reliance on Him. This was clearly the case this past year.

This is the promise God gave to the Laodiceans, "Those whom I love, I reprove and chasten." Why does He do this? To turn us back to Him. To help us avoid the permanent loss of relationship with Him. So, our expectations should be that we will constantly move through this process of testing and purification. When we accept that this is the purification of the narrow way, and embrace that reality, we won't be constantly surprised and disheartened by the experience of what is necessary for our salvation. So, St. Ignatius reveals that we should:

- Assume that life is a constant ebb and flow from consolation to desolation and then back again. This assumption gives us healthy expectations about the future and actually works to reduce the impact and power of the desolation because we expect it.

- Rest when we are in consolation with a peaceful preparation and acceptance of the desolation to come, within which He will give us strength when we enter into that battle.

In contrast to the "rose-colored glasses" distortion, some have a "when is the other shoe going to drop?" negativity about the future. This rule does not point us in that direction. Instead, it is a perspective infused by hope because we understand how God is working in the midst of these ebbs and flows between consolation and desolation. We recognize that His sovereign will allows or causes all things necessary for our salvation. Thus, we can look to the future knowing there will be valleys, but that they have a purpose — not to crush us, but to heal us.

Rule #10: How Should I Act When in Consolation?

Questions for Reflection

* Is the wisdom St. Ignatius provides beginning to help you understand how God works even through desolation and difficulty? If so, how?
* Is this wisdom helping you to deal with the ebb and flow better and to better know how to fight desolation when it comes?
* Are these new realizations helping you to come to peace with the normal process of healing that God invites us to? If so, how?

Rule #11: How Can Humility Help Me Deal with the Ebb and Flow of Consolation and Desolation?

> Let one who is consoled seek to humble himself and lower himself as much as he can, thinking of how little he is capable in the time of desolation without such grace or consolation. On the contrary, let one who is in desolation think that he can do much with God's sufficient grace to resist all his enemies, taking strength in his Creator and Lord.

Humility and abandonment to the will of God in every moment is one of the most powerful weapons at our disposal in our daily spiritual battles for peace. The reason for this is if we are humble, and we are open to whatever the Lord brings, we are thereby attached to very little and the enemy has little room to tempt us. Understanding this, and the normal ebb and flow of consolation and desolation, we can choose to aspire to an attitude of humility at the rise and fall of each.

Accordingly, St. Ignatius tells us how to best pursue humility in this ebb and flow. When in consolation, we should recognize that we had nothing to do with this grace, embrace the consolation with gratitude, and rest in this grace to gain strength as the dawn of desolation emerges. As desolation emerges, the wise pilgrim will deliberately reflect on the fact that God's grace is sufficient, expressing trust in Him to help us to endure the storm and fight against it and through it. We also gain strength in knowing and yielding to the reality that we cannot win the fight in our power, but only His and that He gives us all we need both to endure and win—whatever may be necessary for our salvation.

By now you may have begun to recognize a pattern that all who begin to exercise these battle tactics discover. This pattern follows the path of spiritual maturation that is inevitable when the Paradigm of Ascent™ and the rules of discernment are diligently practiced. The normal path of spiritual maturation is hinted at by St. Ignatius in the shift from the first to the second rule. As a reminder, in the first rule we have someone moving from mortal sin to mortal sin. In the second rule we have someone who is moving from good to better. This is the normative path, but there is far more to it than just these two points of maturation. In fact, the normal path of the Christian spiritual growth is to move from habitual sin to becoming a saint.

What the pilgrim will notice as he begins to become more spiritually mature is that he is less reactive to the stimulus of difficult events in life and the temptation to desolation.

In the first stage of development the pilgrim is often somewhat like an animal when it comes to some stimulus, and the reaction is simply inevitable. For example, in the case of someone who struggles with anger, let's say the event is someone disagreeing with this person and the reaction is an outburst of anger. The event is disagreement, and the reaction is an outburst of anger. There is no self-control. There is almost no ability to avoid the reaction. The event and the reaction are essentially one unfortunate event.

As the pilgrim begins to mature spiritually through the practice of the Paradigm of Ascent™ and discernment of spirits, he begins to notice that his reactions still come but are often separated by a moment, even if extremely brief, where he is able to fight his anger.

Unfortunately, he is not yet strong enough to fight off his inevitable outburst, but as a result of his strengthening Christian faith, he did experience a moment to fight and he did lose the fight in the moment, but he then takes his sin to confession and is both forgiven and gains the strength to fight better in the future. He is also practicing daily mental prayer and developing a deep desire to avoid the damage he causes by his anger.

He prays and asks God for strength to get his emotions under control, and because he is diligent in recognizing when he is in desolation, and less likely to have conflict, he begins to see a change. In this new space between event and reaction he recognizes that the more he fights his reaction, the longer the time between the event and the reaction, and the less severe his outbursts and out-of-control behavior. The connection between event and reaction gets weaker as his faith grows and as his practice of discernment of spirits makes him more aware of the work of the enemy to draw him into sin. His growing self-awareness is also a powerful antidote to falling into sin or even getting into situations that regularly result in sin. This is called avoiding the near occasion of sin.

As he matures even more, he begins to experience a complete break between the event and reaction. In fact, he no longer reacts but simply responds. The difference between a reaction and a response is that a response is a measured expression of the will in submission to God's will regarding how one should comport themselves in the face of any kind of difficult stimulus. Once this process is complete and perfect, at least as perfect as humanly possible, a saint begins to emerge as virtue flourishes and habitual sin is a thing of the past.

The saint doesn't face fewer challenges than the rest of us, the saint is simply more aware and in control of his faculties and better able to manage them according to God's will and the saint's higher nature. Understanding the normal ebb and flow of discernment of spirits, developing a kind of holy God-ward self-awareness, and living the Paradigm of Ascent™ results in a powerful process of maturity and growth in peace.

Questions for Reflection

- Are you beginning to better recognize the ebb and flow of consolation and desolation?
- Are you reacting to the ebb and flow in the same way or are you being purposeful in how you deal with them? If not, are there adjustments you can and should make? What are they?
- Are you seeing a break in the moments where, in the past, you would have simply reacted to desolation or challenging events in life?
- Do you see how your self-awareness is developing? If so, how?

Rule #12: Understanding and Dealing with the Aggression and Threats of the Enemy

The enemy acts like an aggressive dog in being weak when faced with strength and strong when faced with weakness. When an aggressive dog is faced with firm opposition, it loses heart and flees. On the contrary, if the person begins to lose heart and flee, the anger, ferocity, and vengeance of the dog knows no bounds. In the same way it is proper to the enemy to weaken and lose heart, fleeing and ceasing his temptations, when the person who is exercising himself in spiritual things confronts the temptations of the enemy firmly by doing what is diametrically opposed to them. On the contrary, if the person who is exercising himself begins to be afraid and lose heart in suffering the temptations, there is no beast so fierce on the face of the earth as the enemy of human nature in following out his damnable intention with such growing malice.[10]

[10] All of the translations of St. Ignatius's rules are from *Discernment of Spirits* by Fr. Timothy Gallagher. This rule is a variant on Fr. Gallagher's translation that avoids unnecessary distractions

Spiritual Warfare and the Discernment of Spirits

When my two sons Jordan and Ahron were very young they had a Welsh Terrier named Max that was an alpha male. Max was always looking to exert his dominance on anyone he could. Jordan was two years older than Ahron, and Ahron is also autistic. Jordan was more mentally capable and stronger than Ahron. However, Jordan and Ahron dealt with Max in very different ways. One approach worked, and the other didn't. When Max chased Jordan, Jordan had a deeper and natural sense of fear, and Max could smell it a mile away. This happened because Jordan was able to project into the future and consider what a bite might be like. So, Max would approach Jordan with aggressive play, and Jordan, already preconditioned, would turn and run. Things went from bad to worse because Max would bite Jordan's clothing and tackle him, which usually resulted in Jordan yelling for help.

Ahron was a different story. When Max tried to dominate Ahron, Ahron was immediately irritated and responded with a greater fierceness than Max and would often take an angry swipe at him. After a few of these landed, Max decided that he was lower on the totem pole than Ahron and left him alone. Now, obviously the stakes in this humorous game were not very high. However, the stakes of spiritual warfare and the battle for peace and holiness and against sin are as high as heaven and hell.

Have you ever faced an aggressive dog like Max as an adult? Most of us have had this experience. If we were taught well, we should have walked away unscathed, though perhaps shaken depending on the size and strength of the dog. The size and strength of the enemy can be radically larger than ours, but the size and

---

due to St. Ignatius's way of expression. The essence of the rule remains firmly intact.

strength of our God, and God in us, dwarfs the enemy's highest capabilities and powers. Because we know and understand these realities, we can act in a manner that will result in us walking away unscathed rather than dominated.

If you have not been taught well, the wisdom St. Ignatius provides is critical. Here is the breakdown of how this is supposed to work:

- The enemy tries to move us with his aggression.
- When we face him with strength (remember James 4:7), he will back down and flee.
- When we show weakness or turn and run, the anger and ferocity of the enemy grow dramatically and thus his power, influence, and impact on us grow dramatically too.

Regardless of whether we feel it, we must be firm with the enemy and do the exact opposite of what he is attempting to get us to do—the exact opposite of what we feel or desire. Earlier we explored the example of making a commitment to prayer and then when tempted to shorten it or give up, we instead resist and spend more time in prayer. Similarly, the enemy is constantly trying to generate negative emotional energy within us—to get us riled up. As he does this successfully, when we are in the depths of desolation and the heights of anxiety, he then proposes that we do or say something that is in keeping with our lower nature or our normal patterns of sin. To use the example of our previous exploration of anger and the response, when the person is angry or spinning out in anger, the enemy moves the person to act in a way in keeping with their weaknesses and related tendencies, and the patterns of sin in their life.

At this point some of my students tend to get skittish about the battle. Some have asked if they should just not engage in the battle and thus avoid the fight and the possibility of losing. My answer is always the same. The battle is unavoidable. If the enemy can make you fat and lazy by constantly handing you the chips and the remote, he will happily do that for the entirety of your life. He is happy to just stand and guard you and take you gently down the path of sin to hell. If you are not aware of pious tradition in this regard, the saints have often reflected a grave battle they faced with temptation at the end of their lives. The saints win these battles because they have been warriors all their lives. They are strong because they engage. There is no way of avoiding the battle. Either we fight and become stronger, or we avoid and become weaker. Personally, I would rather fight, even if I know I might get beat up, than sit there and allow my spiritual muscles to atrophy so that I can't fight when it is most important. Heaven and hell really are at stake in all of this.

Questions for Reflection

- Have you ever faced down an aggressive dog in the right way? What happened? How did you feel inside? Were you afraid and then faced them anyway?
- Have you ever been tempted to sin and resisted with great energy and won the battle? How did that feel?
- Have you ever been tempted to stay out of this spiritual battle? Is it clear now that this is a very bad strategy? What will you do next time you are tempted?

Rule #13: The Power of Exposing the Enemy's Efforts

Likewise he conducts himself as a false lover in wishing to remain secret and not be revealed. For a dissolute man who, speaking with evil intention, makes dishonorable advances to a daughter of a good father or a wife of a good husband, wishes his words and persuasions to be secret, and the contrary displeases him very much, when the daughter reveals to her father, or the wife to her husband his false words and depraved intention, because he easily perceives that he will not be able to succeed with the undertaking begun. In the same way, when the enemy of human nature brings his wiles and persuasions to the just soul, he wishes and desires that they be received and kept in secret; but when one reveals them to one's good confessor or to another spiritual person, who knows his deceits and malicious designs, it weighs on him very much, because he perceives that he will not be able to succeed with the malicious undertaking he has begun, since his manifest deceits have been revealed.

Spiritual Warfare and the Discernment of Spirits

Demons are creatures. God created and designed them as angels, and through rebellion they fell, and their good characteristics are now warped and distorted. We don't know why some things are as they are with respect to their behavior, but just like humans seeking to do harm, they generally like to work unnoticed. These rules of discernment are like motion-detecting intruder lights on a home. Potential intruders hate the light and will flee the second their attempts to break in can be easily seen as their presence and intent is made known by the light. Now they are more likely to be caught by the police.

Secrecy and isolation are among the most powerful tools of the enemy. With respect to their interaction with humans, demons both tempt and attempt to deceive, and at the same time they work to isolate the one they are working on. When both isolation and other deceptions and manipulations can coincide, their destructive power is magnified. This rule reveals this reality and the remedy is simple and powerful. Turn the lights on! With all the floodlights on, the enemy's power is dramatically diminished, and he will often immediately flee. In this case, turning the lights on is the action of revealing the desolation, anxiety, or related temptation to either a good confessor or a spiritual person.

There is one key to this rule that you must heed in order for it to have the powerful effect that it promises. If this key aspect of the application of the rule is ignored, the lights not only won't come on, but it could get darker and the enemy could end up further entrenched—his power in your life will likely increase. That key is that whomever you reveal your struggle to must be a truly holy person. Ideally, this would mean that they are themselves aggressively moving from good to better, in a state of grace, and at least free from habitual mortal sin. The more holy the person, the brighter and farther-reaching the floodlight you shine on the enemy's work.

In a holy marriage, this can be even more powerful. My wife, Stephanie, and I follow this rule diligently. Though some might caution that I am not the best person for her to reveal her desolation to, she is the holiest person I know. When either of us are in desolation, we simply tell one another. If the desolation is mild, often simply turning on the lights begins to lift the desolation. If the desolation is deep or powerful, then we pray over each other, use holy water, or pray specific deliverance prayers that are suitable for the laity.[11]

With respect to a good confessor, this is probably the best option, especially if they believe in and understand spiritual warfare. However, good priests are often overburdened with many things and not always available on short notice, when the battle is raging. This is why it is best to be a part of a strong Catholic community. There are many good communities where you can find the comradery and support necessary for your spiritual growth and encouragement in times when you are dealing with desolation and temptation to sin. Many of them are third orders, such as the Carmelites or Franciscans. The key is to find one that is faithful to the magisterium and deeply rooted in the traditions of the Church.[12]

---

[11] Fr. Chad Ripperger, Ph.D., *Deliverance Prayers: For Use by the Laity* (n.p.: CreateSpace, 2016).

[12] "Club or Charism" is an article that I have written to help those seeking to find a healthy community and can be found at https://www.apostoliviae.org/resources/10852/club-or-charism.

Questions for Reflection

• Do you have a good confessor to whom you can reveal your battles with desolation?
• Do you have solid friends who are spiritually strong in the Catholic faith who are not gossips and with whom you can share difficult matters like this?
• Have you ever considered joining a faithful Catholic community? Have you done any research about their presence in your diocese or somewhere near you?

Rule #14: How to Strengthen Yourself against Spiritual Attack

> Likewise he conducts himself as a leader, intent upon conquering and robbing what he desires. For, just as a captain and leader of an army in the field, pitching his camp and exploring the fortifications and defenses of a stronghold, attacks it at the weakest point, in the same way the enemy of human nature, roving about, looks in turn at all our theological, cardinal and moral virtues; and where he finds us weakest and most in need for our eternal salvation, there he attacks us and attempts to take us.

Properly understood, desolation is a purposeful, planned, and executed spiritual attack. In this rule St. Ignatius, a former man of war, describes a tactic he probably used when he was leading an assault against an enemy's fort. Here he reveals that the devil conducts himself like a military leader in this kind of situation, seeking to take a specific fort, and that fort is the structure that protects your soul. What is the wall of your fortress made of? How strong is it? How strong of an attack can it withstand?

Spiritual Warfare and the Discernment of Spirits

The enemy pitches his camp to prepare for his assault on you. He watches you day and night without rest, for he needs no rest. He learns your sins, your weaknesses, your proclivities, and your inclinations. With respect to the structure of the fortress around your soul, and the gates of entry, these are the virtues, or lack thereof, in your life. He sends scout demons out to test each gate. They push on them to see if they are strong or weak. If they are weak, the demons take note. Then they go back and make an assessment with the lead demon. They determine your weakest gate, prepare for an assault when you are hungry, angry, tired, or lonely.

The enemy's greatest success will usually be through the gate of your dominant fault or root sin. Your root sin is that one sin that you will wrestle with for the entirety of your life and that will manifest itself in various different ways. In the first epistle of St. John chapter two, he reflects on three root sins: pride, vanity, and sensuality. As a root sin, pride means being attached to our own importance and self-sufficiency. Vanity is being attached to what others think of us. And sensuality in this context means being attached to pleasure, to being comfortable, to the easy way. What makes these root sins is our attachment to something or someone. It's seeking our meaning and fulfillment in something other than God and eternal realities. Later in Church history the classic formula of seven deadly sins emerged and is also helpful in uncovering our root sin. Regardless of the approach, understanding our root sin can help us develop specific elements of our rule of life as discussed in the section on foundations of discernment. If we don't know our sinful tendencies, and the enemy does, we are doubly vulnerable.

St. Teresa of Avila and St. Catherine of Siena both point out that a God-ward self-knowledge is vital to the beginning of a spiritual journey. This kind of self-knowledge is not the kind proffered by pop psychology, but the one that you gain when you are going from good to better. This self-knowledge is an understanding of ourselves that comes when we spend time with Jesus in prayer, when we read and meditate on Scripture, and when we allow the Holy Spirit to speak to us about our sin and God's plan for us. The more you know yourself, truly know yourself, the less vulnerable you will be to the enemy's attacks.

Questions for Reflection

- Do you know what your root sin is?
- Do you go to confession regularly and practice the examen regularly so that you have clarity about your areas of weakness and so that you can remedy them? If not, how do you plan to change this reality?
- Do you have a plan of love or rule of life in place to help you fight this sin and overcome your weaknesses in other areas?

What's Next?

*And I am sure that he who began a good work in you
will bring it to completion at the day of Jesus Christ.*

—Philippians 1:6

If you are like most people of good will, you often read good books
or attend motivating talks, but you are not so satisfied with how
it all plays out in your life. You are not alone; there is a better
way. But first we have several hurdles to overcome with respect
to making your investment in reading this book bear fruit:

- This book is merely a summary of some of the most
  powerful and life-changing truths the Church proposes
  to us. It is a helpful start, but there is so much more
  wisdom and insight available, and that is really necessary
  to make these powerful truths come alive in your life.
- Everyone is in a different place when finishing a book
  like this. For instance, you might struggle with some
  of the basics that we reviewed in the chapter on foundations for discernment. Others might have a sound
  practice of mental prayer but really don't understand
  how to implement a fruitful practice of the examination
  of conscience.

Spiritual Warfare and the Discernment of Spirits

Well, I have good news for you. If you have worked this hard to finish this book, I want to serve you in your new or renewed journey in this battle of faith. Accordingly, I have developed a series of mini-courses for each aspect of this book to help you better understand and live out whatever specific needs you have on this journey. Not only have I made this available to you, but there is no cost. Normally a series of courses on these topics would cost hundreds of dollars at the Avila Institute (which I strongly recommend regardless). However, I really want to make this book and your encounter with these truths a turning point in your life. To take advantage of these courses I have reserved a seat for you at ApostoliViae.com/journey. I pray that you will be deeply blessed by these resources and that your spiritual battle will be won through the One who conquers and heals all in us for the sake of His Kingdom and our salvation.

Regardless of whether or not you decide to take advantage of this powerful formation, be assured that if God is for you, and you engage with His endless well of wisdom and grace in the Church, nothing can stop you on your path to healing and spiritual growth. God and the devil are not equals. The strength of the devil is as a single grain of sand compared to all the sand in the world with respect to God's strength; and this great God is for you. When we begin to avail ourselves of the spiritual weapons and strength He provides, we begin to become a warrior rather than a victim. The presence and power of God grows within us. We move from sinner to saint. This is the call and path of God. Choose this day your destiny in Him, and it will be so. He has promised it to be so, and He is not a liar. You will overcome all the anxiety and damage in your soul. He will heal and strengthen you to become a mighty warrior in His kingdom — to lead others in the face of the storm to Him. You will know the peace that passes all understanding.

As a final recommendation, I would strongly suggest reading this book a second time, asking the Lord to reveal to you which specific spiritual disciplines you need to adopt to move closer to that place where you can know His peace and freedom. If your sacramental foundation is weak, this is the most important place to start. Then comes mental prayer and the examen. Next is ascesis, which is really just living out the previous commitments in a purposeful way. Once you come up with a plan, be sure to focus on just one change at a time, implement that change (by His grace). Once you can achieve your goal at least 90 percent of the time, then add the next discipline. Whatever your area of need, the Avila Foundation and the community of Apostoli Viae provide an endless well of opportunities for formation and spiritual growth. You can find out more about these organizations at:

- SpiritualDirection.com
- Avila-Institute.org
- ApostoliViae.org

As well, don't miss the final section on recommended reading and resources for each area touched upon in this book.

In all of this, remember that you cannot do this on your own. Remember that the difference between a saint and one who remains in a state of mediocrity is that the saint falls a thousand times but gets up every time. He who began this good work in you will be faithful to complete it. Now let's finish this phase of your journey with a prayer:

Most glorious, kind, and blessed God of the present moment, I beg Your grace and Your presence that I might be able to reject the temptations of the enemy and my flesh that drive my mind to obsess on the past or worry about the future. Help me instead to embrace the sufferings and challenges of the present moment knowing that You are with me in them and that if I surrender myself to You and the duties of this present moment, You will give me all I need to endure or overcome any challenge, take care of all matters that are outside of my control, and will reveal Yourself and Your holy will within and through them. By Your grace I reject, in Jesus' name, all regrets, laments, frustrations, or other temptations that draw my thoughts and attention away from the duties of this present moment and more importantly, away from Your presence and provision. I affirm, invoke, and implore the power of Jesus' name against the efforts of the enemy to draw me out of Your presence in this moment, and I, by God's Grace, His Divine Will, and my human will, through the power of the Holy Spirit, choose to take every thought captive to the obedience of Christ. Mary, Mother of the Divine Will, pray for me.

Recommended Resources for Continued Spiritual Growth

As a special offer for those who are ready to more deeply engage in the battle for peace and strength in the storm, if you go to ApostoliViae.org/journey and register, I will provide you with a series of free mini-courses on discernment of spirits, mental prayer, the examen, and much more. As well, you will gain access to a summary guide that you can print out for both the examen and the rules of discernment that will reinforce what you have read in this book and help you to learn and apply the powerful life-changing wisdom of St. Ignatius of Loyola. Below you will also find a list of recommended resources to help you on your journey.

Daily Spiritual Sustenance

SpiritualDirection.com is a website that has the central purpose of helping you to grow spiritually by providing thousands of articles, videos, and other powerful materials rooted in the magisterium-faithful mystical tradition of the Church. Be sure to sign up for our daily email that will provide you with new insights on the journey every week.

Spiritual Warfare and the Discernment of Spirits

Targeted Formation (for busy people and those who have a bit more time on their hands)

Avila Institute for Spiritual Formation (Avila-Institute.org). The Avila Institute provides spiritual formation to laity, priests, and religious worldwide through live online classes. These studies are both at a level for busy people or graduate studies for those who have the time.

Prayer

Into the Deep—Finding Peace Through Prayer, by Dan Burke is the simplest, most straightforward book in print on how to begin or deepen your prayer life (SpiritualDirection.com/shop).

Finding God Through Meditation, by St. Peter of Alcantara, is a book that will help those who have practiced mental prayer daily for some time to dive deeper into prayer and devotion. St. Peter was a spiritual director to the great mystic St. Teresa of Avila (SpiritualDirection.com/shop).

Rule of Life and Root Sin
Identification and Mitigation

Navigating the Interior Life—Spiritual Direction and the Journey to God, by Dan Burke, provides an understanding of how to grow spiritually with or without a spiritual director (SpiritualDirection.com/shop).

The Seven Deadly Sins: A Thomistic Guide to Vanquishing Vice and Sin, by Kevin Vost, is a very accessible and practical treatment of understanding sin and how to overcome it (SpiritualDirection.com/shop).

Spiritual Combat, by Lorenzo Scupoli, will provide more wisdom on how to overcome sin and grow spiritually. This book was perpetually with St. Francis de Sales and regularly promoted by him (SpiritualDirection.com/shop).

Sacraments

Confession: Its Fruitful Practice is a very brief but powerful guide to the fruitful practice of confession (TANBooks.com).

A Devotional Journey into the Mass, by Christopher Carstens, will help any committed Catholic learn how to enter more deeply into the mysteries of the Holy Sacrifice of the Mass (SophiaInstitute.com).

Discernment of Spirits

Sacred Story Affirmations: Meditations on Discernment of Spirits, by Fr. William Watson, S.J.

Sacred Story: An Ignatian Examen for the Third Millennium, by Fr. William Watson, S.J., will provide the reader with a deep path of reflection and healing through the wisdom of St. Ignatius (Sacredstory.net).

The Discernment of Spirits, by Fr. Timothy Gallagher, O.M.V., is an extraordinary work dedicated to providing an in-depth and practical understanding of St. Ignatius's teaching on Discernment of Spirits (Crossroadpublishing.com).

More on Finding Peace

Searching for and Maintaining Peace, by Fr. Jacques Philippe, is a very brief but powerful reflection on how to find and maintain peace (Scepterpublishers.org).

Spiritual Warfare and the Discernment of Spirits

The Sacrament of the Present Moment, by Jean-Pierre de Caussade (translated by Kitty Muggeridge), is a powerful reflection on the providence of God and how He works in and through all events of life. This book is indispensable for those seeking to deepen their abandonment to God and know His peace (HarperCollins).

About the Author

Dan Burke is the president and chief operating officer of EWTN News, Inc. In his deep commitment to the advancement of faithful Catholic spirituality, he is also the founder and president of the Avila Institute for Spiritual Formation, which offers graduate and personal enrichment studies in spiritual theology to priests, religious, and laity in seventy-two countries and prepares men for seminary in fourteen dioceses.

Dan is the author and editor of more than fourteen books on authentic Catholic spirituality and, with his wife, Stephanie, hosts the *Divine Intimacy Radio* show, which is broadcast weekly on EWTN Radio. Past episodes can be found, along with thousands of articles on the interior life, at SpiritualDirection.com.

Most importantly, Dan is a blessed husband, father of four, and grandfather of one—and is grateful to be Catholic.

SPIRITUAL DIRECTION
⤜ SERIES ⤛

SOPHIA INSTITUTE PRESS

If this book has caused a stir in your heart to continue to pursue your relationship with God, we invite you to explore two extraordinary resources, SpiritualDirection.com and the Avila Institute for Spiritual Formation.

The readers of SpiritualDirection.com reside in almost every country of the world where hearts yearn for God. It is the world's most popular English site dedicated to authentic Catholic spirituality.

The Students of the Avila Institute for Spiritual Formation sit at the feet of the rich and deep well of the wisdom of the saints.

You can find more about the Avila Institute at
WWW.AVILA-INSTITUTE.COM.

Sophia Institute

Sophia Institute is a nonprofit institution that seeks to nurture the spiritual, moral, and cultural life of souls and to spread the Gospel of Christ in conformity with the authentic teachings of the Roman Catholic Church.

Sophia Institute Press fulfills this mission by offering translations, reprints, and new publications that afford readers a rich source of the enduring wisdom of mankind.

Sophia Institute also operates the popular online resource CatholicExchange.com. *Catholic Exchange* provides world news from a Catholic perspective as well as daily devotionals and articles that will help readers to grow in holiness and live a life consistent with the teachings of the Church.

In 2013, Sophia Institute launched Sophia Institute for Teachers to renew and rebuild Catholic culture through service to Catholic education. With the goal of nurturing the spiritual, moral, and cultural life of souls, and an abiding respect for the role and work of teachers, we strive to provide materials and programs that are at once enlightening to the mind and ennobling to the heart; faithful and complete, as well as useful and practical.

Sophia Institute gratefully recognizes the Solidarity Association for preserving and encouraging the growth of our apostolate over the course of many years. Without their generous and timely support, this book would not be in your hands.

www.SophiaInstitute.com
www.CatholicExchange.com
www.SophiaInstituteforTeachers.org

Special Thanks to Our Lauch Team

A. Michael Boggs; Abigail Rodriguez; Al and Pat Elsenpeter; Alex Ancheta; Alexandra Kubebatu; Allison Ricciardi; Allison Russo; Amber Whitehead; AMGD; Amy Curtis and Family; Amy Fenner; Amy Gilmore; Amy Holmes, OCDS; Amy Hooper; Andrea Boring; Andrew Kosmowski; Anita; Ann Marie; Ann Marie Alvey; Ann Therese Harrison; Ann Virnig; Anna Dajero; Anna Janina Gromek; Anna Marie S. Lopez; Anne M. Keller; Anne Tschanz; Annette Kos; Anthony Cammarata; Anthony Guerrero; Anthony Pecora; Antonio Vito Gioiello; Antonio Zebedeo Abad; Augustine Fredrich; Aurore Chartier; Barbara Devries; Barbara Isemann; Barbara Zupcsan; Becky Malmquist; Berkeley Monroe; Bernadette; Bernard Chinnasami; Beth Whittaker; Bill; Bill and Margaret Whitehead; Bill Jeffries; Bill LaMay; Biz Blee; Bob Lebida; Bonita Erickson; Bournemouth Oratorians; Brad and Gerri Rupp; Bradley; Brenda Sinkovitz; Brenda Stevens; Brett Van Vuren; Bridget G. McGill; Bridget Spitznagel; Bryon Herbel; Candace MacMillan; Carla Paola Cosentino; Carla Rowland; Carlos De Quesada; Carmen Andrade; Carmen Diaz; Carmen Doudna; Carol; Carol A. Durkin; Carol and Larry Lintner; Carol Joyce; Carol Rebecca Slade; Carol S. Bugglin, Ph.D.; Carolyn Herring; Carolyn Homan; Carrie Anderson; Catherine F. Price; Catherine Lins; Catherine Minor; Cathleen Ludlow; Catholic Life Institute; Cathrine, Sophie, and Emma; Cathy Carson; Cathy Hammock; Cathy Trowbridge; Cathy Urlaub; Cecilia A. Torres; Cecilia Marks; Charlene; Charlotte Hollis; Chris; Chris Tuthill; Chris, Caroline, and Ben; Christa Oancia; Christina A. Gomez; Christina M. Carlos; Christine Rich; Christine Sharmila Rego; Christopher A. Jachulski; Christopher Castagnoli; Christopher Landfried; Christopher Ricketts; Christy Remorin; Chuck and Betsy Stokes; Cindee Hodges; Cindi Peyton; Cindy; Cindy; Claire Dwyer; Claire Garland; Claire Swift; Clare J. Crone; Claudia Bouhaidar; Claudia Grams; Clint Ufford; Colleen Cronin; Colleen Morrison; Colleen Walker; Connie Wieczorek; Constance Prescott;

Cornel S. Gray; Craig Savio; Cris and Jeff Davis; Cristina Contreras; Crystal Hernandez; Curt Hamilton; Cynthia Melstrom; Cynthia Oberschlake; Cynthia Ramirez; Cynthia Snider, OCDS; D. Trom; D.F.W.; Daisy Jane Lor; Dana Deboer; Dana F. Grout; Daniel Salazar; Danielle Bozaan; Danielle Therese George; Darlene Gilbeau; David Gardner; David Raju, Jr.; David W. Warner; Dawn Marie Roeder; Dawn Powell; Deacon Barney Lejeune, In Memory of Andrea Lejeune; Deacon Dan; Deacon Gary Simmons; Deacon Greg Sass; Deacon Gus and Veronica Salazar; Deacon Jim and Anne McLevey; Deacon Joseph Bell; Deacon Mike Strain; Deacon Scott Sowell; Deacon Tom Fox; Dean Huff; Deanna Scheffe; Deb Egan; Debbie Aguiar; Debbie Gargano; Debbie Real; Deborah Densmore; Deborah Rodriguez; Deborah S. Gordon; Debra Goff-Liegghio; Debra Mcpherson; Denise Andrin; Devanie Marie Cooper; Diana L. Ruzicka, RN, MSN; Diana von Glahn; Diane Roe; Diane Sanders; Diane Sowell; Dione Therese; Dolores Ann Dever; Dom and Maggie Cingoranelli; Don and Susan Pelletier; Dona Gray; Donna Le; Donna M. Ottaviano-Britt; Donna Mcsoley; Donna Saavedra; Donna Stanley; Doreen Patricia Moisey; Douglas Rofrano; Dr. Amada Lim; Dr. and Mrs. Brett Maddux; Dr. Carol Younger; Dr. Daniel Sherban; Dr. Nancy Williamson; Duane Albert; Dylan Jedlovec; E. E. Segura; E. L. Catherine; Edward and Lady Carmel Cole; Edward Breen; Elaine Knight; Elisa A. Lopez; Elisa Redmond; Elizabeth; Elizabeth Block; Elizabeth Foll; Elizabeth Rozycki; Ellen Carney; Emily Wilford; Eric Armando Francis Gaitan; Eric S. Austin; Erica Shepherd; Erik Acheff; Erik Winkelmann; Estela Tackie; Ester Munt-Brooks; Ezekiel Cristobal-Addison; Father Arun; Father Chris Decker; Father Ian Jeremiah; Father Kevin Morris; Father Michael Goyette; Father Robert Bustamante; Father Samuel Speringl; Father Stephen P. Moran; Father Todd petersen; Father William G Waun, Ph.D.; Felix and Soledad Arroyo; Flordeliza Verzosa; Frances Garcia; Frank Ciarcia; Gail A. Patterson; Gary A. Boice; Gary Capone; Gene Kelly; Geoffrey Cunningham; George Miller; Geraldine Marie Soileau; Gilbert Snodgrass; Glenn and Cammi Dickinson; Greg; Greg Delozier; Gregory Cravetz;

Gregory Fernandes; Gregory Laroux; Griselda Garza; Harry L. Colin; Harry Ohmstede; Heather J. Combs; Hector Rodriguez (KofC); Helen Cool; Helen Joseph; Helen L. Smith; Helen Young; Holly Parsons; Hope D. Aspengren; Ida Vigil-Otis; In Memory of Dorothea Gomez; In Memory of My Late Husband, Josef Weirathmueller; In Memory of Paul Kummet; In Memory of Raymond and Del Shenoha; Ina Carr; Irene Robertson; Isabelle D'Souza Quin; J. A. Mead; J. Wales; Jack E. Collins; Jacqueline Chambaz; Jacquelyn Moore Warren; Jakov Perisa; James Wilson; Jana Cirincione; Janet; Janet Fuller; Janet N. Wray; Janet Tan; Janice; Jason; Jean Occhialini; Jeanette Woodley; Jeanne Knotts; Jeannette Barbacane; Jeff Mire; Jeff Walker; Jeffrey Linard; Jeffrey S. Crane; Jeniffer; Jennie G. Buhs; Jennifer B. Hilderbrand; Jennifer Brown; Jennifer Densch; Jennifer Roney; Jennifer Whitsett; Jenny Mansingh; Jeremy Hazuka; Jesus Rego; Jhoe Stonestreet; Jill Flood; Jillian Buhl; Jillian Danelle (Duff) Wernke; Jim and Jolene Garcia; Jim and Paula Cosgrove; Jim Como; Jim Dotterweich; Joan Richardson; Joann Vellara; Joanne Campuzano; Joe and Mary Ann Renna; Joe and Nicole Vogle and Family; Joe Humphrey; Joe Leal; John and Kathy Maddox; John and Lydia Raschke; John and Susanne Scatliff; John Bennett; John C. Ivan; John Kennedy; John McCaffrey; John Miner; John P. Witiuk; Jonathan Hoyt; Jordan Burke; Jorge Medina; Jose Erubel Rios; Jose Santos; Joseph; Joseph Alcruz; Joseph and Mary Pronechen; Joseph Cardali; Joseph Myers; Joseph Rich; Joseph Sinnott; Joseph Tenaglia; Josh Meeker; Joy Pinto; Juan Baca, Jr.; Judie Van Pevenage; Judy Longoria; Judy Silhan; Julie Allison; Julie Casey; Julie E. Perez; Julie Habiger; Julie Scegura; Karen; Karen; Karen Bianco; Karen Burden; Karen Defrees; Karen G. Davidian; Karen Graff; Karen Hynds; Karen Theresa Olsen, OP; Karleen Smith; Kathleen Gloria Beckman; Kathleen Johnson; Kathleen Wright; Kathryn Buskey; Kathryn Hammen; Kathryn Therese Mulderink; Kathy Brouillette; Kathy Stefanov; Katie Kuchar; Keith and Patricia; Keith R. Smith; Kenneth and Patricia Horstman; Kenneth Donajkowski; Kent Zieser; Kevin M. Davey; Kevin Vost; Kevin Wells; Kim; Kim Pearse; Kimberly Kenson, OFS; Kimberly Pizzuto; Krisann Gilbert;

Kristi Klawitter; Kristian Kaveto Mana; Kristin Priola; Kristin Wilson; Kylene Wesner, Ph.D.; Lamont Applegate; Latens Vita; Laura Ashley Maurizzi; Laura Haymes; Laura Heater; Laura T. Daniel; Laura Weller; Lauren Dickie; Lauri; Leah Ann Phillips; Leasa Yoshida; Leif Gardner; Leonard E. Wathen, Jr.; Leticia "Lety" Lopez; Linda A. Jones; Linda M. Crowley; Linda M. Fentner; Linda Petote Martin; Linda Rofrano; Linda Ugwuonah; Linda White; Lindsey Fankhauser; Lisa; Lisa Christensen; Lisa Ferguson; Lisa M. Frederick; Lisa Marie Bald; Lisa Pleskach; Liza Sama; Logan Amster; Lori A. Irlbeck; Lori Brison; Lori Hamrock; Lori Kananen, LMC; Lori Sautter; Luan Morrow; Lucy Smyth; Luisa Acosta; Lupe Yasutake; Lynda Rozell aka Tin Can Pilgrim; Lynn H. Simpkins; Lynne Fischer; M. Troxell; Madeleine M. Addy; Maggie Herd; Major and Mrs. Michael Bannon; Mandy Marie Goulet-Addy; Marc Wood; Margaret Antonetti; Margaret E. Honore; Margaret Motzel; Margaret Seguin; Margarita Carreon-De Alba; Maria Aznar; Maria Guadalupe Ramirez; Maria Mesarosova; Marian Howlett; Marian Mazzone; Marianne; Marie Ann Morrison; Marie Bateh; Marie Richards; Mariel Lafleur De Soleil Lafleur; Marilyn Dayton; Marilyn K. Baker; Marion Conn; Marion Douglas; Marissa Mendoza; Marjorie Arni; Mark and Christine Martinez; Mark and Julie Seegers; Mark Lindberg; Mark Wetzel; Marlene M. Mulford; Marlon De La Torre; Marta Chacon; Martha Luke; Martha Martinez; Martha Sherman; Mary Ann; Mary B. Underwood; Mary Carol Joyce; Mary Eileen Stackley; Mary Ellen Durkin; Mary Ellen Jackson; Mary F. Gerber; Mary Ireland; Mary Jean; Mary Jeanne Stronks; Mary L. Ridder; Mary L. Sealy, COL. USA (ret); Mary M. Lawrence; Mary Morgan; Mary Peltier; Mary Reichel; Mary Roberta Charlesworth; Mary Treinen; Mary W. Jank; Mary, Terri, and Sarah; Maryann Fay; MaryAnne Moran; Matthew and Marya Pouliot; Matthew Cobb; Matthew Gonzalez; Matthew J. Novak; Matthew Jacobson; Maximillian Amster; Meg and Max; Meg Clark; Melinda Beyer; Melissa Brown; Melissa Overmyer; Michael and Sarah Vacca; Michael J. Bartkoski; Michael J. Slusz; Michael JP Daly; Michael Keenan; Michael Knapp; Michael Mulski, KCHS; Michael Patrick Woods;

Michael Vitz; Michele Dirks; Michele Perez; Michele Thompson; Michelle; Michelle Griffith; Michelle Long; Miguel and Cristina Acosta; Miguel Perez; Mike and Laurie Gold; Mike Dixon; Milagros Diaz Jackson; Mim Mouton; Minh Nguyen Lisa; Mirek Kolinko; Mona Allen; Monica Dolenc; Monica Ludwig; Mr. and Mrs. Edwin R. Rose, Jr.; Mr. P. Downing; Mrs. Laura Warthen; Mrs. Martha Richardson, OFS; Mrs. Parke Raffensperger; Nadine Metling; Nalina Chinnasami; Nancy Lowney DeBacker; Nancy Marlin; Nancy Mathias; Nancy Sanders; Nate Jones; Nenita Tan; NIcholas and Marie Ustick; Nicholas Russell; Nick and Lori; Nina Cardillo; Nina Polchlopek-Gardner; Nissa Chadwick; Noah and Crystal Friend; Noel Phillips; Norman D. Harvey; Onyl; Pamela Burns Dolney; Pat Moroney; Patrice Cigallio Wesa; Patrice Guidry; Patricia Blake; Patricia Fanning; Patricia Palmer; Patricia Yamrick; Patrick Brown; Patrick Cummings; Patti and Leif Gardner; Patti J. Smith; Patty Brewer; Patty Turbak; Paul and Christina Semmens; Paul Okuja; Paul Star; Paula Campopiano; Peg Watson Ebert; Peggy Angstadt; Peggy M. Mouton; Peggy Maggio; Peggy Meyer; Peggy N. Hool; Penn Herbert; Peter Anninos; Peter J. Witiuk; Phil Fleming; Phil Milan; Philip Clingerman, OCDS; Phillip A. Bellini; Phyllis Horning; Pilar B. Carbajo; Preston and Janice Ritchie, My Beloved Deceased Wife; Rachel Watson; Rainer 'Ray' Knoblauch; Ralph Delgiorno; Raymond P. Moczulski, M.D.; Regimol Joseph; Renee Frost; Rev. Bro Francis Philip Downing; Rev. Fr. Celestine Nwakwuo, OP; Rev. Peter Di Tomasso; Rex and Barbara Sanders; Rhonda A. Hall; Rhonda Hayes; Rich Rochelle; Rich Slan; Richard Isaac Roland; Richard Marshall; Richard Murray; Richard Paine; Richard Slusz; Rick Rieger; Rita and Joe Lane; Rita K. Levine; Rita M. Liebegott; Robert A. Griffin; Robert E. Davis; Robert Sempijja; Robin Sellers; Rodney Harris; Roger and Karen; Ron Schrader; Ronald Couture; Rosa M. Mendoza; Rose Greer; Ross Hansen; Rotji Pali; S. Waguespack; Sally and Scott; Sally Victoriano; Sandra Geist; Sara McIntosh; Sara Zervos; Sarah Driver; Scott French; Sean; Shane; Shannon Sykes; Sharon Semtner; Shelly Hogan Shebib; Shelly M. Haynes; Sheri Jampo; Sheryl Sotero; Sheryl Zavertnik;

Sister John Patrick; Sister Madelyn Louttit; Sister Mary Magdalene Prewitt; Sisters of Mary, Mother of the Church; Sita Vasan; Sr. Florence Suimin. OSA . England.; Stephanie A. Mann; Stephanie Ann Ortiz; Stephanie Loegering; Stephen Berry; Stephen Rice; Stephen Skowronski; Steve and Ann Weaver; Steve Foose; Steve Solimene; Subdeacon Dennis Somerville; Sue Cote; Sue Werner; Sue Wunder; Susan Bryan; Susan Cuzelis; Susan EM Heroux; Susan Frechette; Susan J. Brown; Susan Jacobsen; Susan King; Susan Schuler; Susan Scott; Susan Skinner; Susan Tolson; Suzie Vendetti; Sylvia Rook; Tammie Randall; Tammy Palubicki; Tara Kamann; Tere Adams; Teresa McReynolds; Teresa Richter; Teresa Wells; Terrance and Mary Betthauser; Terry L. Cook; Tesa Fleming; The Crain Family; The Henwood Family; The Lawrence Family; The Miller Family; The Musalem Family; The Olmstead and Ellsworth Families; The Ortega Family; The Paris Family; The Quintana Family; The V. Willett Family; The Williams Family; Theresa Brown; Theresa Getzwiller; Therese Allgeier; Thomas Digiovanni; Tim Becker; Tim Connelly; Tim Hanavan; Timothy Suter; Tina Marie Lefebvre; Tina Tocco; Tom and Lisa Buss; Tom Dwyer; Tom Reichert; Tomas Voboril; Tony Kerr; Trevor Trumbull; Trish Pesyna; Troy J. Lawson, Sr.; Valerie Gaudet; VeraLucia Cottim-Coughlan; Vicki Oberle; Vicki Woods; Vickie Newell; Vikki Lasota; Vince and Shellda Monterosso; Virginia Boland; Virginia Fitzhugh-Lee; Vonnie; Walter Wakefield; Wilfred Gomes; William A. Bennett and Mary L. Bennett; William A. Curry; William Kreider; William Steffen; Yalile G-Deal; Yvette Melancon; Zachry Page; Zlatko Sram